MONOGRAPHS OF THE
SOCIETY FOR RESEARCH IN
CHILD DEVELOPMENT

Serial No. 249, Vol. 62, No. 1, 1997

A LONGITUDINAL TWIN STUDY
OF INTELLIGENCE IN
THE SECOND YEAR

J. Steven Reznick
Robin Corley
JoAnn Robinson

WITH COMMENTARY BY
Adam P. Matheny Jr.

MONOGRAPHS OF THE SOCIETY FOR RESEARCH IN CHILD DEVELOPMENT
Serial No. 249, Vol. 62, No. 1, 1997

CONTENTS

COMMENTARY

ABSTRACT

Reznick, J. Steven; Corley, Robin; and Robinson, JoAnn. A Longitudinal Twin Study of Intelligence in the Second Year. With Commentary by Adam P. Matheny Jr. *Monographs of the Society for Research in Child Development,* 1997, **62**(1, Serial No. 249).

Data from 408 pairs of identical and same-sex fraternal twins assessed at home and in the laboratory at 14, 20, and 24 months are used to describe cognitive development in the second year and to identify genetic and environmental influences on phenotypic similarity. The primary dependent variables are the Bayley Mental Development Index and separate constructs (based on items from the Bayley and the Sequenced Inventory of Communication Development) to measure nonverbal ability, expressive language, and receptive language. These variables are supplemented with laboratory tests of word comprehension, visual attentiveness, and memory for locations.

Various patterns of development emerge for separate constructs, for females versus males on each construct, and for individuals across constructs. These data suggest developmental transitions for many infants during the second year, but the timing of these transitions varies by measure. The dependent variables tend to be intercorrelated and are reasonably stable for individuals, with greater stability late in the second year, suggesting either increasing stability or more effective measurement. Expressive and receptive language scores are correlated and have comparable patterns of change within individuals, but there are also differences (e.g., receptive language accounts for the most variance in MDI at each age and across ages). There are genetic effects on MDI at each age and effects of shared environment at 20 and 24 months.

Analyses of separate constructs reveal distinct patterns. Effects on nonverbal abilities are entirely genetic. Effects on language are primarily environmental, but genetic influence emerges for expressive language at 20 and 24 months and for receptive language at 14 months. Visual attentiveness tended to reveal effects comparable to the nonverbal construct, and word comprehension was related to the receptive composite. Scores on the memory for locations task were relatively uninformative. A Cholesky decomposition is used to identify influences that account for the same variance at each age (i.e., promote continuity) and that account for new variance at each assessment (i.e., promote change) and to explore overlap and distinctiveness among measures at each age.

I. INTRODUCTION

The second year of human life is characterized by dramatic transitions in all domains of psychological development, but there is broad consensus that psychologists know less about the second year than any other phase of the life span (Bronson, 1985; Carew, 1980; Kagan, 1981; Shatz, 1994). One reason for this lacuna is that children between the ages of 1 and 2 are notoriously difficult to test. Younger infants respond in predictable, almost automatic ways in various research paradigms (e.g., they stare at novel stimuli), and older children comprehend instructions and can thus be encouraged to perform specific tasks. During the second year, the child is increasingly autonomous but not yet guided reliably by instruction. A second reason for our lack of knowledge about the second year is that many hotly debated questions apply either to younger or to older children. For example, research on the earliest manifestations of memory, expectations, and the understanding of physical laws is mainly pertinent to the first year. Traditional research on the child's knowledge of conservation, causality, or the mental states of others tends to use paradigms in which the child answers questions, so this research is mainly conducted with children older than 2 years. Our goal in the present project was to explore main effects and individual differences in the development of intelligence during the second year.

The rich tapestry of behavior in the second year is composed of various threads that can be labeled *cognitive, motoric, emotional, temperamental,* and *social,* but the term *intelligence* is generally used to denote actions that require thinking, memory, problem solving, categorization, language, or other mental abilities. These actions often depend on motoric ability as well (i.e., the neuromotor capacity to execute a plan, perform a task, pronounce a syllable). However, this aspect of development is generally ignored when the research focus is intellectual behavior and the motoric abilities that are required are well within the competence of most children in the focal age range. Temperament, emotion, and sociability are involved in intelligent behavior as well in the sense that a child must have some motivation to perform a given task and that the child's personality will influence his or her response to the exam-

1

iner, to the testing context, to success, and to failure in ways that affect cognitive performance. These influences can be explored (e.g., Birns & Golden, 1972; Matheny, 1989; Matheny, Dolan, & Wilson, 1976; McCall, Eichorn, & Hogarty, 1977; Petrill & Thompson, 1993; Slomkowski, Nelson, Dunn, & Plomin, 1992) but are often ignored given the rationalization of regarding them as peripheral sources of error that are minimized when tests are engineered to be effective measures of cognitive competence. Our strategy here will be to focus relatively narrowly on cognitive abilities.

Within the domain of actions that require thinking, memory, problem solving, categorization, language, or other mental abilities, there is a long-standing debate concerning whether intelligence is best viewed as a unitary general capacity (Spearman, 1904; Stern, 1914) or as a set of separable abilities (Guilford, 1967; Thompson, 1919; Thorndike, 1914; Thurstone, 1938). Principal components analysis often suggests a single general factor across subtests, neurological mechanisms can be posited that could affect a range of cognitive variables (e.g., density of axonal and dendritic processes, efficacy of synapses, speed of neural conduction), and general intelligence has been an effective predictor of various outcomes (e.g., school performance). However, pioneering work by James McKeen Cattell (described in Kendler, 1987) and other, more recent efforts to define intelligence emphasize separable aspects, such as linguistic, spatial, and logical-mathematical intelligence (e.g., Gardner, 1983; Sternberg, 1977). We see no reason to participate in this debate—it seems obvious to us that there is practical and theoretical utility in defining intelligence as both a general competence and a set of separate abilities. In our opinion, a description of intelligence that does not include unitary and componential views is simply incomplete. The challenge is to find a defensible conceptualization and measurement strategy that will allow us to assess general intelligence and components of intelligence during the second year.[1]

Most research on child development emphasizes either developmental function or individual differences (Cronbach, 1957; McCall, 1981; McCall et al., 1977; Wohlwill, 1973), and both approaches can be applied to variables that are quantitative or qualitative (Emmerich, 1964; McCall, 1981). Developmental function refers to change and continuity over time in the values of a given attribute. For example, as normal infants get older, they produce an increasingly large number of words. The quantitative function for vocabulary acquisition could follow any form, with levels of vocabulary over time indicating periods of continuous growth, accelerated growth, quiescence, or decline. Quantitative developmental function could be represented as a graph of the species-typical function for vocabulary over time or as an equation with appro-

[1] For a broad overview of contemporary issues regarding the nature of intelligence, see Neisser et al. (1996).

priate parameters. *Qualitative developmental function* refers to a succession of different age-specific stages or plateaus in the infant's ability. For example, under normal circumstances, young infants babble, 1-year-olds say single words, and 2-year-olds produce some two-word combinations. Qualitative developmental function could be visualized as a series of age-specific charts, each containing a set of bars for babbling, single words, and two-word combinations. The height of each bar would indicate the percentage of infants who could be categorized into that stage of language at that particular age.

Development of individual differences refers to the relative rank order among individuals on a given attribute. A correspondence between rank orderings over time indicates stability; the lack of correspondence indicates instability. Quantitative measures of individual differences are common. For example, the rank ordering of infants in their productive vocabulary at 1 year may or may not correspond to their rank ordering on productive vocabulary at subsequent ages. This relation can be visualized as a scatter plot with vocabulary at year 1 on one axis and vocabulary at a subsequent year on the other. It is also possible to characterize individual differences at a particular age on the basis of a qualitative variable. For example, Bates, Bretherton, and Snyder (1988), Nelson (1973), and others have noted that children have various strategies for engaging in language (e.g., referential children name things, expressive children participate in conversation). Stability of qualitative developmental function implies that individual children maintain the same strategy across time. This relation can be visualized as a set of cross-classification tables in which each child is categorized as expressive or referential at Time 1 and recategorized as expressive or referential at a subsequent time.

In this *Monograph*, we use the developmental function approach and the individual differences approach to explore qualitative and quantitative aspects of the development of intelligence during the second year. Developmental function is not generally relevant for the study of normal intelligence because intelligence tests are designed to mask developmental changes in mental ability (i.e., the content of test questions shifts with age). However, the assessment of developmental function is well established in the study of some components of intelligence (e.g., changes in memory ability [Diamond, 1985]; changes in expressive vocabulary [Goldfield & Reznick, 1990; Gopnik & Meltzoff, 1987; Nelson, 1973]). The analyses of developmental function and individual differences will be conducted for the cohort as a whole and separately for males and females. Thus, one focus in the present *Monograph* is to explore developmental transition, but with a net broad enough to capture various aspects of transition across groups and across variables.

The fact that intelligence has a particular developmental function or that individual differences are more or less stable may establish a description of development in the second year, but a more fundamental question looms: Can mechanisms be adduced to account for these effects? We would need to know far more psychology and biology to identify specific causal mechanisms to explain qualitative or quantitative developmental function or differences among individuals. However, we can begin this account in broad strokes with reference to environmental and genetic influences. All organisms develop in some environment and are affected by a particular genetic heritage, so neither influence can be ignored. However, for any particular ability at any particular age, the data may suggest that environmental or genetic influences provide a more compelling account of phenotypic variance. Also, for any particular ability, environment and genetics may play different roles in their effect on developmental function and individual differences and may have differential effects on continuity and change over time.

We will address these questions with data from an ongoing longitudinal twin study. Given certain assumptions about twins, these data can be used to explore general questions about developmental function and individual difference, but their greater value emerges for the identification of genetic and environmental influences. The methodology of behavioral genetics allows us to explore the relative importance of genetic and environmental influence on measurements at particular assessment ages and also to identify influences that promote continuity and change over time and overlap and distinctiveness across measures. The mathematical and statistical techniques that support these inferences will be described in detail below.

Our approach here is multilevel in that we will decompose the construct *intellectual development* into general and specific measures and the construct *children* into species-general statements and results for boys and girls. Also, we will explore questions of developmental function as well as individual differences. We are particularly interested in the effects of environment and heredity. We will decompose these effects into influences on a particular measure at a particular age, influences on the continuity and change of a particular measure over time, and influences on the overlap and distinctiveness across measures at a particular age.

This multilevel approach has advantages and disadvantages. The main advantage is realism: global measures of intellectual behavior offer a view of the developing child that is no more or no less valid than the view afforded by more specific measures; generalizations about the average child can mask individual and subgroup differences that have both theoretical and practical significance; and the relative weighting of genetic and environmental influences that affect children on a particular measure at a particular age may not be the same as the weightings of genetic and environmental influences on continuity and change over time or on overlap and distinctiveness across measures. The main disadvantage to a multilevel approach is a loss of parsimony. Some attractive coherences may emerge across levels of analysis and across measures, but nature is seldom that generous. Given the complexity of most psychological phenomena, it seems unlikely that the disparate set of processes that support intellectual ability will undergo a unidimensional transition at a single point in time or be affected by a genome or an environment that is monolithically efficacious across groups and individuals. Thus, the modal product from a multilevel approach is likely to be complicated and inconsistent.

We believe that this untidy story or "essential messiness" (Kessen, 1984) is preferable because it is more realistic, but we note the need for caution in its interpretation. Given a finite set of resources for gathering a sample of research participants and performing psychological measurements on those participants, every bifurcation in grouping or measurement causes a reduction in power or resolution. Specifically, a sample composed of just boys or just girls will be more variable than a sample composed of all children, a cross-age analysis will have more missing data than an analysis at any particular age, and subscores from a multi-item test will have more variability than a general score derived from all items.

In the following introductory chapters, we will first describe the Bayley Mental Development Inventory (MDI), which is a primary assessment procedure in this study, describe developmental functions and individual differences that are revealed by the MDI, and review how the MDI is affected by genetic and environmental influences. We will then describe efforts to partition MDI items into separable constructs. From this perspective, we will defend our strategy for identifying the aspects of intelligence that we label *expressive language, receptive language,* and *nonverbal abilities,* and we will discuss previous findings relevant to these constructs. Finally, we will describe two additional nonverbal abilities that were assessed in the present study: memory for locations and visual attentiveness.

II. INTELLIGENCE AS A GENERAL ABILITY

The most widely known efforts to observe and describe intellectual behaviors in toddlers emerged in the early decades of the twentieth century. The widespread interest in adult intelligence crossed paths with the child study movement, and early intelligence tests were introduced (e.g., the Gesell Test [Gesell, 1925, 1928], the Cattell Mental Test for Infants and Young Children [Cattell, 1940], and the Griffiths Scale [Griffiths, 1954]).[2] Several of these tests confounded mental ability with motor ability, and few are in wide use today. We will focus on one intelligence test that does separate mental and motor ability and that is generally regarded as the best general measure of early development currently available (Sattler, 1990)—the California First Year Mental Scale developed by Nancy Bayley (1933), now known as the Bayley Scales of Infant Development (BSID; Bayley, 1969). (A second edition of the BSID—the BSID-2—was introduced in 1993, several years after the present study had begun.)

The BSID is composed of items (i.e., specific contexts in which infant behavior is observed and categorized) grouped into two sets: a set of 81 motor items (e.g., crawling, climbing stairs) and a set of 163 mental items (e.g., response to sound, imitation, visual discrimination, memory, problem solving, language comprehension, and language production). The BSID is a "power test" (Anastasi, 1976): normative research was conducted to determine the age at which most infants respond correctly to each item, and items in the final test are ordered by tenths of months according to this age-based expectation. Raw scores calculated on the basis of the number of passed and failed items are converted into a Psychomotor Development Index (PDI) and a Mental Development Index (MDI), which are normalized standard scores derived from a national stratified sample of normal infants and children. The BSID also provides scales for rating various dimensions of temperament, emotion, and test-taking behavior.

[2] For a detailed description of this period, see Brooks and Weinraub (1976), Colombo (1993), or Dunst (1978).

CONTINUITY AND CHANGE IN DEVELOPMENTAL FUNCTION

Intelligence is assessed in the MDI through the use of items that require the child to perform activities that are generally considered intellectual (i.e., thinking, memory, problem solving, categorization, language, or other mental capacities). However, the main developmentally relevant information in the MDI (and other infant intelligence tests as well) is in the arrangement of test items to reflect a normative chronology of accomplishment in which an individual's performance can be evaluated relative to expectations for same-aged peers. The fact that individual differences in test scores will be preserved across time assures the MDI's practical relevance (e.g., to identify children whose mental performance is notably advanced or retarded compared with their peers) but makes it less than satisfying as a tool for studying developmental function. To the extent that the MDI items have been chosen appropriately and that the normative data are representative, there should be no general change in an individual's MDI over time. Some children may show a systematic change in MDI because of emerging poor health, recovery from previous poor health, or other circumstances (e.g., color blindness would become relevant on the MDI only in late infancy), but, for most normally developing children, the MDI should hover at about the same level over time.

The norm-oriented design of the BSID guarantees that age-to-age change in MDI score will not reveal quantitative developmental change (i.e., a general pattern of growth or decline in MDI score over time). However, longitudinal data from the MDI have been used to identify changes in qualitative developmental function. McCall et al. (1977) explored the items that compose the first principal component (i.e., the set of items that cluster as the most salient characteristic across a group of subjects) in the California First Year Mental Scale data from subjects in the Berkeley Growth Study. These analyses suggested notable changes in the composition of the first principal component at 2, 8, 13, 21, and 30–36 months. For example, after 13 months, items entered the first principal component that seemed to reflect the child's acquisition of expressive language and ability to perform nonverbal tasks (e.g., put blocks in holes). After 21 months, the first principal component was dominated by items related to expressive and receptive language, with additional items related to nonverbal abilities. These shifts in continuity of the qualitative developmental function co-occurred with periods of instability in individual differences, which led McCall et al. to posit the presence of successive stages of development. These stages can be criticized on various methodological and statistical grounds (e.g., the MDI scores were well above average, suggesting a nonrepresentative sample; conclusions often differed for males and females; the sample size was relatively small; and month-to-month stability and instability were not defined statistically). However, as will be described later, there are various other perspectives that also suggest notable change in development during the second year.

STABILITY AND INSTABILITY OF INDIVIDUAL DIFFERENCES

In the present context, we are particularly interested in the persistence of individual differences across the second year. Wilson (1983) reports correlations for the MDI of .56 between 12 and 18 months, .48 between 12 and 24 months, and .67 between 18 and 24 months for 350–400 participants in the Louisville Twin Study. Other studies report comparable coefficients. For example, Siegel (1981) found correlations for the MDI of .65 between 12 and 18 months, .59 between 12 and 24 months, and .73 between 18 and 24 months for 148 full-term and preterm singletons. These values suggest strong stability, particularly in the context of the MDI's test-retest agreement, which is estimated to be between .76 and .80 (Spreen & Strauss, 1991; Thompson, Fagan, & Fulker, 1991). Furthermore, the greater stability for the 6-month intervals between 12, 18, and 24 months than for the 12-month interval between 12 and 24 months suggests the underlying structure of a quasi-simplex model, which can be defined as a matrix of correlations with large values adjacent to the principal diagonal (i.e., at adjacent ages) and with a reduction in the size of correlations as distance from the diagonal increases (i.e., as the gap between two ages becomes larger). Humphreys and Davey (1988) demonstrated the adequacy of this model to describe measures of intelligence from 1 to 9 years. To summarize, there is considerable stability in intellectual ability as measured by the MDI but also considerable instability (i.e., over half the variance between successive MDI scores is unaccounted for).

GENETIC AND ENVIRONMENTAL INFLUENCES

Relatively little is known about genetic or environmental influences on developmental function or individual differences in general measures of intelligence during the second year. The idea that intelligence has heritable influences dates from the ancient Greek philosophers, but it had its most formal modern expression in Darwin's theory of biological evolution (Darwin, 1859) and was studied in detail by Galton (1883, 1869/1962). The importance of environmental influence has a rich philosophical and psychological heritage (e.g., Locke, Helmholtz, and Watson; for a review, see Kimble, 1993) but became particularly salient in the context of the plight of institutionalized children (Goldfarb, 1943) and controversy about affecting intelligence through enriching the environment (Goodenough, 1939; Simpson, 1939; Wellman, 1932).

All humans and their close relatives (e.g., the chimpanzee) share the majority of their genome (Vigilant, Stoneking, Harpending, Hawkes, & Wilson, 1991). Genetic variability in behavior occurs when people carry different alleles of a gene at a particular locus influencing behavior. Thus, we use the term *genetic influence* to describe variance in the small minority of genes that are polymorphic (i.e., that have different alleles) and that affect behavior (cf. Wahlsten, 1994).

The relative role of genetic and environmental influence on intelligence might be resolved through analysis of adopted children, for, in this circumstance, the correlation that is usually present between genotype and environment is reduced or absent. Adoption studies indicate that intelligence scores for adopted children are correlated with intelligence scores for biological parents and for adoptive parents—Bouchard and McGue (1981) estimate these correlations as .22 and .19, respectively, which is roughly half the magnitude of the average correlation between parents and offspring (Bouchard and McGue report a value of .42 on the basis of over 8,000 pairs). It is difficult to estimate heritability precisely in the adoption design because of such problems as assortative mating, selective placement, and genotype-environment correlation and interaction (see Turkheimer, 1991), but these data converge on the conclusion that, for a wide range of ages, IQ scores are affected by heritable and environmental influences (Plomin, DeFries, & McClearn, 1990).

This pattern could change with age. For example, genetic and environmental effects in adoption studies for infants in the second year are relatively weak. Plomin and Defries (1985) review studies reporting IQ correlations for biological mothers and their infants given up for adoption, and they report a range of values between −.01 and .09. These studies did not provide correlations between adopted children and adoptive parents, so environmental effects cannot be assessed, but the data suggest that genetic effects as revealed by adoption studies are modest during the second year. More recent data are available from the Colorado Adoption Project, which includes longitudinal data from adopted children, their biological parents, their adopted parents, and their adopted siblings. The parent-offspring correlations from this study (for both biological parents pooled) are .14 and .12 at 12 and 24 months, the parent-adoptee correlations .09 and .05, and the nonadopted control correlations .05 and .14 (Fulker, DeFries, & Plomin, 1988). The magnitude of these effects is small, but, as Plomin (1986) notes, the genetic relation between parent and offspring requires both heritability and an age-to-age genetic correlation (i.e., genetic variance in infancy must be correlated with genetic variance in adulthood). From this perspective, although the parent-offspring correlation is small, it implies significant heritability and genetic correlation.

Twin studies offer a second perspective on genetic and environmental effects on intelligence by comparing monozygotic (MZ) twins to dizygotic (DZ) twins. MZ twins have a 100% chance of sharing any relevant alleles found in their co-twin. DZ twins (and siblings) are considered 50% similar genetically in the sense that there is a 50% chance that relevant alleles can be traced back to a common ancestor. That is, the chance that both twins (or siblings) share a particular allele from their father is $.5 \times .5 = .25$, and the chance of sharing an allele from their mother is $.5 \times .5 = .25$. These two probabilities sum to .50, which reflects the probability of tracing any shared psychologically relevant allele back to a parent (Plomin, DeFries, & McClearn, 1990). In contrast, it is often assumed that twins who are reared together, be they MZ or DZ, have the same degree of shared environment. Under the traditional assumptions of Mendelian genetics, the difference between the MZ twin correlation and 1.0 can be attributed to influences that impinge on one twin and not the other. This quantity is called *unique,* or *nonshared, environment* and is labeled e^2. The difference between the MZ twin correlation and the DZ twin correlation reflects half the variance that can be accounted for by shared genetic effects (i.e., it is a contrast between pairs sharing 100% of their genes and pairs sharing 50% of their genes). To account for the full genetic effect (labeled h^2), the difference between the MZ twin correlation and the DZ twin correlation is doubled. Finally, the MZ twin correlation minus the genetic variance reflects the variance that can be accounted for by shared environment. The effect of shared environment is labeled c^2.

Estimates of heritability and environmental influences can be affected by violations of various assumptions of the behavioral genetic model (discussed in detail below; see also Goldsmith, 1993; Wahlsten, 1994). The most salient effect of violating these assumptions is to complicate the comparison of influences measured with different samples, with different instruments, or in different laboratories. However, for a series of measures collected longitudinally, or for similar measures obtained at the same time, the relative magnitudes of MZ-DZ twin differences can provide valuable information about genetic and environmental influences across time and across measures (McGue, Bouchard, Iacono, & Lykken, 1993).

Before we review the data from twin studies, note that some implementations of the adoption design afford a similar analysis. For example, the design used in the Colorado Adoption Project allows a comparison of correlations between adopted siblings, whose shared identity by descent is 0%, and non-adopted siblings, whose genetic similarity is 50% (as explained earlier). The number of pairs is relatively small (between 61 and 82 pairs at 12 and 24 months) but would allow the detection of large effects. Plomin, DeFries, and Fulker (1988) report MDI correlations for nonadoptive and adoptive pairs of, respectively, .37 and .03 at 12 months and .42 and .12 at 24 months. This pattern of correlations suggests strong genetic effects and negligible environmental effects.

The Louisville Twin Study has been an important source of data on the development of MZ and DZ twins. Data from approximately 100 pairs of MZ twins and 100 pairs of DZ twins assessed longitudinally reveal MDI correlations for MZ and DZ twins of, respectively, .68 and .63 at 12 months, .82 and .65 at 18 months, and .81 and .73 at 24 months. These data suggest h^2 values of .10, .34, and .16, respectively (Wilson, 1983), and strong effects of shared environment. At 18 months and older, the MZ within-pair variance was significantly less than the DZ within-pair variance. These data support the conclusion that there are significant but modest genetic effects on individual differences in general intelligence as measured using the MDI during the second year. Indeed, Louisville Twin Study twin correlations for general intelligence at 24 months equal or exceed the values generally reported for adults, which can be quantified as median twin correlations of approximately .80 for MZ pairs and .60 for DZ pairs (Bouchard & McGue, 1981; Loehlin & Nichols, 1976; McCartney, Harris, & Bernieri, 1990; McGue et al., 1993). The comparison of these values suggests that roughly half the observed variation in general intelligence in adult humans and older infants is associated with genetic influence.

Finally, when data from adopted and nonadopted siblings are combined with longitudinal data from twins, effects of heredity and environment can be estimated using sophisticated path models. Cardon, Fulker, DeFries, and Plomin (1992) and Fulker, Cherny, and Cardon (1993) combined data from children in the Colorado Adoption Project with data from the Twin-Infant Project (DiLalla et al., 1990) and a subset of the subjects described below. They found heritability estimates of .51–.55 and .60–.68 at 12 and 24 months and shared environment estimates of .11–.12 at 12 months and .18 at 24 months.

These findings suggest some heritable influence on intelligence in the second year, although there are discrepancies: heritability estimates in the Louisville data are low when compared with estimates from the Colorado Adoption Project and the Twin-Infant Project. Also, the pattern of change in the age-specific influence of h^2 is unclear: some data suggest increasing influence, and other data suggest a more variable pattern. Effects of shared environment are also discrepant: estimates from the Colorado Adoption Project and the Twin-Infant Project are low compared with estimates from the Louisville Twin Study. MDI scores for a large sample of MZ and DZ twins at 14, 20, and 24 months could help resolve these differences.

CONTINUITY AND CHANGE IN GENETIC AND ENVIRONMENTAL INFLUENCE

The genetic and environmental effects discussed earlier were age specific. That is, estimates of h^2, c^2, and e^2 at a particular age indicate the extent

11

to which these influences account for phenotypic variance at specific points in time. From this perspective, the relevance of development is that the relative importance of influences might change over time. For example, individual differences in intelligence might become increasingly affected by a genetic influence. One limitation of this approach is that it is based on a between-group effect, even when calculated using longitudinal data. This model fits McCall's characterization of analyses in most developmental studies as "the parametric study of immature organisms" (McCall, 1981, p. 2).

From a developmental perspective, genes and environment might affect continuity and change in phenotypic variance.[3] That is, a genetic or environmental influence might contribute to phenotypic variance for an extended period of time and thus promote continuity. In contrast, some other genetic or environmental influence might contribute to phenotypic variance at a specific age or for a constrained period of time and thus promote change. These sorts of influences can be identified and quantified in models applied to longitudinal data on twins or adoptees.

Various approaches are available for modeling the effects of continuity and change. For example, Wilson (1983) found that there is greater synchrony in the patterns of spurts and lags in the cognitive development of MZ twins in the Louisville Twin Study, which suggests a genetic influence on continuity and change. Cardon et al. (1992) and Fulker et al. (1993) used path models applied to various sources of data (described earlier) and found that the genetic variation present at 12 months is expressed at 24 months but that additional genetic variation is also introduced at 24 months. In contrast, the influence of shared environment is associated with continuity between 12 and 24 months, and the effects of unique environment are time specific. Plomin et al. (1993) used change scores and co-twin cross-time correlations, supplemented with more sophisticated longitudinal model-fitting analyses of MDI scores, for a subset of the present sample at 14 and 20 months and found comparable results for genetic influences (i.e., effects on continuity and change) and unique environment (i.e., change) but also found that shared environment influenced both continuity and change. Finally, Cherny, Fulker, Emde, et al. (1994) used a Cholesky model (this approach is described in detail below) to explore continuity and change in MDI scores for the present cohort at 14, 20, and 24 months. The pattern of effects replicated Cardon et al. (1992) and Fulker et al. (1993): a genetic influence promoting continuity across the second year but an additional genetic effect promoting change at 24 months; a single shared environment effect promoting continuity across the second year; and a series of age-specific effects for unique environment.

This pattern of results for continuity and change on the MDI is reason-

---

[3] For a thorough introduction to this theme, see Plomin (1986).

able and informative. There is variation in performance on all psychological indices, but the source of this variance can change over time. In the present context, genetically coded products or environmental effects could have varying influence across task or across time. The models described earlier attempt to attribute variance at Time 1 to specific sources (i.e., genetic, shared environment, unique environment) and then to determine whether the sources of variance at Time 1 are the same sources that account for variance at subsequent times (i.e., whether there is continuity) and also whether additional sources of variance are implied (i.e., whether there is change). The results indicate genetic influences on both continuity and change in MDI scores. Genetic continuity could emerge on the basis of neurological configuration, fundamental processing skills, temperament, motivation, or any other trait that affects performance on the MDI. Change at 24 months (and not at 20 months) implies that one or more genetically coded products begin to claim additional variance late in the second year. The continuous effect of shared environment suggests some stable aspect of the environment that affects performance (e.g., responsive parents, age-appropriate toys, well-maintained diurnal schedules). Finally, the age-specific effect of unique environment is reasonable because this source includes the effects of unreliability of measurement, which should be time specific, and the effects of transient environmental influences, such as illness or mood.

It is important to distinguish between efforts to partition variance into specific sources identified as genetic or environmental and efforts to determine whether the influences of these sources over time are identical (i.e., whether there is continuity) or different (i.e., whether there is change). In the former case, the sources of variance are mutually constraining in the sense that they must sum to 100%: if two effects are large, the third must be small. Given that variance is not standardized across time, the influence of the three sources could increase in absolute magnitude yet remain constant in proportion. In contrast, designations of continuity and change in the sources that influence variance are not mutually constraining. The proportion of influence that we designate as genetic can be constant across time, but the influence can be considered either identical (continuity across time) or different (change across time), or both, depending on the pattern of cross-twin and cross-time relations. Moreover, the detection of new genetic influences at 24 months does not preclude continuity with genetic influences important at earlier ages.

III. SEPARABLE ASPECTS OF EARLY INTELLIGENCE

Despite the fact that the BSID provides a single score reflecting mental development, Bayley did not conceptualize intelligence as a unitary, general capacity. Rather, she posited the successive emergence of complex mental processes or sets of processes, with each growing out of, but not necessarily correlated with, previous processes (Bayley, 1933, 1970). This pattern of change in intellectual ability creates periods of continuity and of discontinuity in qualitative developmental function, as discussed earlier. The difficult problem is to identify the sets of processes that characterize the intellectual ability of infants at various ages.

EMPIRICAL APPROACHES

One approach to identifying the processes that characterize an infant's mental ability at a specific age is to factor analyze BSID Mental Scale items, but there is some question how these factors should be interpreted. A factor analysis of the MDI items reveals the items (or sets of items) that are most strongly related to the overall MDI. These items emerge because they evoke individual differences at a particular age: items that are well within or far beyond the child's competence serve no diagnostic purpose. There are two practical implications of this fact.

First, a factor analysis of MDI items reveals items that are relevant for diagnosing individual differences among infants at a particular age but not necessarily for detecting the abilities that best characterize the infant in any general sense. For example, by 14 months, almost all infants will say "da-da" or its equivalent. This tendency to apply simple names is a salient characteristic of 14-month-olds, but this item generates little variance among that age group and is therefore unlikely to emerge in a factor that reflects individual differences. There is more variability in the 14-month-old's ability to name an object presented by the examiner, and therefore this item is likely to be included in a factor. By 24 months, the tendency to name things is a salient characteristic of the child, and almost all infants will name an object presented by the examiner. But, because there is no longer variability in the item, it is no longer likely to be included in a factor.

Second, the items that compose a factor are drawn from the subset of items that are age appropriate, not the broader set of all possible items. Other items that tap this same ability but that are too hard or too easy will not be administered and cannot participate in the factor. Thus, the set of items that emerge as a factor is not a factor in the traditional sense of a cluster of related items that are a distinguishable component of a larger group of items. Rather, that set is a cluster of related items that constitute a distinguishable component within the subset of items *diagnostic of individual differences and typically administered* at a particular age.

Despite these limitations, factor analysis of the MDI can be informative. Hofstaetter (1954) used data on the California First Year Mental Scale, a forerunner of the BSID, collected longitudinally from 2 months to 18 years in the Berkeley Growth Study and identified a potent but vaguely interpretable factor present between 2 and 21 months, which he labeled *sensorimotor alertness*. Cronbach (1967) subsequently questioned Hofstaetter's approach and offered analyses that cautioned against the factoring of age-to-age correlations. Stott and Ball (1965) undertook an extensive age-specific factor analysis of items from the 12-month California First Year Mental Scale and several other infant intelligence tests, and they identified factors that could be labeled (in contemporary terms) *fine motor, expressive language, goal-directed behavior,* and *memory*.

More recently, Lewis, Jaskir, and Enright (1986) used principal components and oblique factor rotation analysis to generate separate, nonorthogonal factors across MDI items for children tested longitudinally across the first 3 years of life. Three factors emerged at 12 months and were labeled *means-end, imitation,* and *verbal skill*. Four factors emerged at 24 months and were labeled *lexical, spatial, verbal symbolic,* and *imitation*. Burns, Burns, and Kabacoff (1992) reported a factor analysis on MDI items from infants at these same ages, but different factors emerged, such as *fine motor, language,* and *memory* at 12 months and *language, form board* (one of the BSID test materials), and *interactive behavior* at 24 months. Finally, Gyurke, Lynch, Lagasse, and Lipsitt (1992) reported MDI factors labeled *fine motor, perceptual/motor,* and *language* at 12 months and *language, fine motor,* and *problem solving* at 18 months.

The components of early cognitive development that emerge in these factor analyses differ across studies but do suggest that sets of items that reflect individual differences in cognitive ability during the second year can be conceptualized within a general bifurcation into verbal and nonverbal domains. Nonverbal components can be separated further into specific abilities, such as memory, imitation, and problem solving. A fine motor component also emerges in several studies.

15

There is one additional approach to factor analysis of BSID items that would seem to be useful. When the BSID is repeated regularly and frequently, the longitudinal data that result can be recast to reveal the age at which each child first passes each item. This score has the advantage of allowing any pair of test items to correlate despite differences in the average age at which the items are passed. Bayley (1970) reported a factor analysis on the age of first pass for children tested longitudinally in the Berkeley Growth Study (monthly from 1 to 15 months and then trimonthly to 36 months) with items drawn from the California First Year Mental Scale and the California Preschool Mental Scale. Factor analysis revealed 12 factors (six on each test), but only seven factors had items assessed in the second year: perceptual interest, vocal communications, meaningful object relations, perceptual discrimination, object relations, memory for forms, and verbal knowledge. Thus, in this alternative approach, the same factors reported earlier emerged. Moreover, the problem stated earlier still remains: the analysis of average age at which the items are passed reveals the set of items that tend to be passed at the same age, not the set of items that measure the same underlying construct.

A second approach to defining subsets of related test items is to impose them on the basis of theoretical considerations. Bayley used this strategy in her initial segregation of the BSID into mental and motor items on the implicit theory that the items within each of these two domains tap abilities that seem similar. Indeed, the recent revision of the BSID uses theoretical and empirical methodology to subdivide MDI items into four facets: *cognitive, language, social,* and *motor.* Other test developers also segregate items. For example, the Gesell Developmental Schedules contain items grouped into the categories *motor behavior, adaptive behavior, language behavior,* and *personality–social behavior* (Gesell, 1925, 1928), and the Griffiths Scale (Griffiths, 1954) is divided into *locomotor, personal-social, hearing and speech, hand and eye development,* and *performance* subscales.

THEORETICAL APPROACHES

Several researchers have proposed schemes for subdividing the mental items of the BSID into theoretically defined subsets. For example, in a study of the scalogram properties of the MDI for infants aged 1–27 months, Kohen-Raz (1967) identified subsets of items, each assumed to measure a definitive function of infant behavior. These subsets, derived from the work of Gesell, Griffiths, and Piaget, were labeled *eye-hand, manipulation, object relation, imitation/comprehension,* and *vocalization/social contact/active vocabulary.* Yarrow, Rubenstein, and Pedersen (1975) used a similar approach, grouping MDI items according to the class of response elicited, the cognitive function tapped, or the most relevant psychological processes. Their analysis included only items relevant for the first year of life, but some similar categories emerged, including *vocalization and language, object permanence, visually directed reaching and grasping,* and several categories of motoric ability. More recently, Dale, Bates, Reznick, and Morisset (1989) sorted items on the BSID for 20-month-old infants into three subsets with theoretical coherence: items that require *expressive language skills,* which is related to the Kohen-Raz vocalization/social contact/active vocabulary subset; items that require *receptive language skills,* which is related to the Kohen-Raz imitation/comprehension subset; and *nonverbal items,* which combines elements of the remaining Kohen-Raz subsets.

IV. EXPRESSIVE AND RECEPTIVE LEXICAL ABILITY AS ASPECTS OF INTELLIGENCE

In this *Monograph,* we will embrace the Dale et al. (1989) division of the MDI into three constructs. Thus, we are obliged to defend the theoretical integrity of each construct, a task that is most straightforward for the measures of expressive and receptive lexical ability. The goal of this description of expressive and receptive aspects of language is to suggest that it is relatively easy, and theoretically important, to identify the sorts of behaviors that children engage in that indicate ability in these two domains.

Factor analyses of general tests of infant intelligence often suggest the utility of segregating items into verbal and nonverbal domains, and the principal components analysis reported by McCall et al. (1977) indicated that expressive language ability is a salient source of individual differences early in the second year and at around 21 months. The Piagetian account of cognitive development did not focus on language per se, but other theorists (e.g., Bruner, 1973; Kagan, 1981; Shatz, 1994; Vygotsky, 1962) have noted the critical role that language plays in the toddler's cognitive development. Moreover, attention to the verbal aspects of intelligence is particularly warranted because psycholinguistic accounts of development often focus on changes during the second year (e.g., Bates et al., 1988; Brown, 1973); because measures of infant information processing often correlate with later linguistic competence (Fagan & McGrath, 1981; Rose, Feldman, Wallace, & Cohen, 1991; Tamis-LeMonda & Bornstein, 1989; Thompson et al., 1991); and because language ability in older children is often highly correlated with measures of intelligence (Rose & Feldman, 1995; Terman, 1918; Wechsler, 1949).

Most English-speaking 2-year-olds have begun to produce and comprehend some multiword utterances, but language development in the second year is primarily reflected in the child's acquisition of a lexicon. Relevant items on the BSID are primarily about the child's ability to name objects or pictures or to respond to more or less familiar referents or complex commands. There is ongoing debate about the appropriate description of the psychological mechanisms that underlie expressive and receptive lexical ability, but it seems likely that both require a cross-domain mapping between representations.

Receptive lexical ability refers to the child's knowledge about the association between signs (i.e., words and gestures) and objects, events, or internal states. Receptive abilities generally emerge between 8 and 10 months and are inferred when the child responds to linguistic commands with appropriate behaviors (e.g., stops activity in response to "no-no," orients to his or her own name, or looks at a dog when asked to "look at the dog"). Checklist-based parent reports of receptive language suggest that 12-month-olds comprehend an average of 80 words (Fenson et al., 1993). Extrapolating from the rate of growth that is evident in the second year, the comprehension vocabulary at 24 months would be extremely large. Behaviors that indicate receptive ability in older infants also include appropriate linguistic responses.

Expressive lexical ability refers to the child's tendency to use verbalizations (and, in many accounts, gestures) to affect an ongoing interaction or to refer to present or absent objects or events. Expressive language can be observed directly when the child says a word in the context of a particular game, says a word in response to a particular prompt, or says a word spontaneously. Most early words are supported by ritualized games or routines (e.g., saying "woof woof" in response to a toy dog). Checklist-based parent reports of expressive language indicate that 14-month-olds produce an average of 10 words and that 24-month-olds have an average productive vocabulary of 324 words (Fenson et al., 1993), but there are vast individual differences (i.e., the norms range between 2 and 163 words at 14 months and between 48 and 647 words at 24 months; see also Bates et al., 1994; Fenson et al., 1994).

Comprehension emerges in most infants several months before production (Fenson et al., 1993; Harris, Yeeles, Chasin, & Oakley, 1995; Ingram, 1974), and the infant's receptive vocabulary is estimated to be 5–10 times larger than the expressive vocabulary (Benedict, 1979; Fenson et al., 1993). This suggests some discrepancy between these two aspects of the lexicon, but other studies suggest similarities. Totals for receptive and expressive vocabulary tend to be correlated when measured via observation (Nelson, 1973; Slomkowski et al., 1992) or parent report (Reznick, 1990; Tamis-LeMonda & Bornstein, 1990); there is evidence of periods of marked acceleration in both domains for many children (Reznick & Goldfield, 1992); and word use (e.g., contextual flexibility) is similar in comprehension and production (Harris et al., 1995). Similarity between expressive and receptive vocabulary seems reasonable in that both domains depend on the child's capacity to learn from incoming speech (Huttenlocher, Haight, Bryk, Seltzer, & Lyons, 1991) and both domains require the same (or similar) representational mappings (i.e., a stored representation that can be triggered by some past, current, or future state of affairs and used to program a phonological or manual response).

19

Despite the obvious similarities between the expressive and the receptive lexicons, there are empirical and theoretical reasons for separating them. Thal and her colleagues (Thal & Bates, 1988; Thal, Tobias, & Morrison, 1991) report that many children with delays in expressive language have normal scores for receptive language. This dissociation between receptive and expressive vocabulary can also occur for children at the other end of the developmental spectrum. Bates, Thal, and Janowsky (1992) report that some children with advanced ability in expressive language have normal receptive language. This somewhat mysterious discrepancy between expressive and receptive language could occur if children produce words without comprehending them (Leonard, Newhoff, & Fey, 1980), but the more likely explanation is that these children produce a relatively large proportion of the words they comprehend (i.e., they say all that they know) whereas most normal children produce only a small proportion of the words they comprehend. Other dissociations between the expressive and the receptive lexicons include differences in the percentage of nominals in the two domains (Behrend, 1988; Fremgen & Fay, 1980) and different degrees of overextension in comprehension and production (Thompson & Chapman, 1977).

Peripheral processes may have unique effects on either aspect of language. Expressive language requires planning (e.g., taking in adequate breath to produce audible utterances) and phonological output and can be affected by a temperamental disposition toward either a hesitancy or a compulsion to talk. Receptive language requires phonological input, and its assessment will generally be affected by the child's motivation and compliance. Finally, the distinction between expressive and receptive language can be applied to the verbal ability of older children and adults. Sincoff and Sternberg (1987) draw a distinction between verbal comprehension, which is required for reading and listening, and verbal fluency, which is required for writing and speaking. Comprehension and fluency are intercorrelated but emerge as separate components in a principal components factor analysis of verbal tasks with elementary-school-aged children.

These dissociations (particularly the double dissociation between early and late talkers) suggest the existence of two distinct mental or neural mechanisms (Bates et al., 1992). Comparable conclusions also emerge from the study of children with focal lesions (Bates, Dale, & Thal, 1995), and neurological disorders have been identified that have selective effects on expressive or receptive language (e.g., Broca's aphasia, Wernicke's aphasia). It is beyond the scope of the present investigation to propose descriptions of these separable mechanisms, but the distinction between expressive and receptive abilities seems clear and is likely to be relevant in an account of psychological development in the second year.

CHANGE AND CONTINUITY IN DEVELOPMENTAL FUNCTION

Qualitative developmental function for language could be viewed in various ways, but recent research suggests the utility of defining specific styles of language acquisition. For example, Nelson (1973) describes children as referential if their earliest words are object names (e.g., *dog*) and expressive if their early vocabulary makes more use of personal-social routines and formulas (e.g., *up*). Bloom (1970) draws a distinction between children who use nominal and pronominal grammatical forms, and Bates et al. (1988) compare an analytic approach with a holistic approach to language.[4] The measures of the expressive and receptive lexicons that we use in this study do not provide a view of any well-known language styles but do allow us to compare relative ability in the expressive and the receptive domains.

Quantitative change in the developmental function for expressive language in the second year is well established. Expressive language emerges for most infants shortly before the first birthday and increases dramatically by the end of the second year. For many infants, this increase takes the form of a spurt in productive vocabulary, marked by a dramatic change from an earlier, slower rate of acquisition (Bates et al., 1988; Bloom, 1973; Gopnik & Meltzoff, 1987; McCarthy, 1954; Nelson, 1973). Onset of the spurt is often midway to late in the second year, but spurt onset may vary considerably depending on differences in assessment technique, definition of the spurt, and such individual characteristics as sex and birth order. Goldfield and Reznick (1990) found that some children show other patterns of expressive language development: some children have a relatively continuous pattern of growth that leads to a comparable level of vocabulary; other children seem to acquire expressive language very slowly, saying few words at all during the second year.

Given the association between at least some aspects of production and comprehension, it seems reasonable to expect that receptive language will show similar patterns of quantitative developmental function, yet this hypothesis has received little attention. Benedict (1979) reports comprehension scores for individual children early in the second year. Inspection of her figure 1 suggests the possibility of differentially timed comprehension spurts. Oviatt (1980, 1982) found a significant increase in comprehension ability at about 17 or 18 months, but stimuli were new representations of a recently learned stimulus, and this does not necessarily imply a general spurt in comprehension. Recently, Reznick and Goldfield (1992) found a significant correspondence between the presence and the timing of spurts in production and comprehension.

---

[4] For a review of these and other language styles, see Shore (1995).

STABILITY AND INSTABILITY OF INDIVIDUAL DIFFERENCES

Individual differences in language acquisition during the second year have been investigated for two decades, but, as noted earlier, the primary focus of this work has been the identification of the particular paths or approaches that individual children use to acquire language. In this *Monograph*, we explore two facets of the individual differences issue. First, we can determine whether individual differences in expressive and receptive ability are stable across the second year and whether these two aspects of language are related. We are not aware of data on the stability of individual differences in production or comprehension, but, as noted earlier, there is reason to suspect that these domains are related. Second, we can determine whether expressive language and receptive language are related to contemporary and future intellectual performance. This latter facet builds on work by Bates et al. (1988) and Rescorla (1984), in which receptive ability early in the second year predicted general linguistic and intellectual development at ages 2–3.

GENETIC AND ENVIRONMENTAL INFLUENCES

Disorders of speech and language, such as developmental dyslexia and stuttering, appear to be heritable (DeFries, 1985; Howie, 1981; Lewis, Ekelman, & Aram, 1989; Lewis & Thompson, 1992; Pennington & Smith, 1983; Tallal, Ross, & Curtiss, 1989), but most models of normal language development focus on environmental mediators, such as input from parents. This environmental orientation predominates despite the fact that correlational studies usually confound environmental influence with genetic influence. For example, Lieven (1978) reports that mothers who are verbally responsive and engage in more dialogue have children who do a great deal of labeling and describing of objects (i.e., a referential style), and Goldfield (1993) reports that mothers who more often label toys during play have children who learn more nouns. Note that these effects could be mediated through the linguistic environment that the mother provides, through aspects of the child that evoke language-relevant behavioral tendencies in mothers, or through a heterotypic genetic mechanism that induces infants to prefer nouns and that induces mothers to provide labels.

Huttenlocher et al. (1991) investigated these effects by comparing various indices of language input with growth rates for expressive vocabulary in the second year (defined as a quadratic function fit to each child's spontaneous utterances recorded at 2- or 4-month intervals). Their findings indicate that mothers who speak more have children who acquire vocabulary faster. Moreover, the relative frequency of specific words in mothers' speech is related to the order in which their children acquire those words. Huttenlocher et al. argue against child-driven causality: the quality of mothers' speech does not change across the second year (see also Nelson & Bonvillian, 1973; Smolak & Weinraub, 1983), and child-driven causality is not a plausible explanation for the effect of word frequency. However, as Huttenlocher et al. note, their results do not preclude the possibility of substantial genetic effects.

The data from adoption studies suggest some genetic effect on early language. Hardy-Brown, Plomin, and DeFries (1981) used a full adoption design to contrast the effects of heredity and environment on language in 1-year-old children. Children's communicative performance (defined as the first principal factor across a variety of linguistic measures, such as vocalization, gesture, imitation, and phonological ability) was affected by aspects of the behavior of their adoptive mother but even more so by the cognitive abilities of their birth mother, suggesting genetic influence on language production in the first year. Hardy-Brown and Plomin (1985) reanalyzed these data in comparison with nonadoptive control families and replicated the finding that infant communicative competence is significantly related to the general cognitive ability of the birth mother, not the adoptive parents. This additional analysis also revealed that some language variables that could be attributed to the mother (e.g., the tendency to imitate the infant's vocalizations) were related to infant communicative competence in both adoptive and nonadoptive homes but that others (e.g., the frequency of question sentences) were related only in nonadoptive homes.

These different patterns of correlation suggest that some aspects of the home environment may be mediated by genetic factors shared by parent and child. Plomin et al. (1988) calculated separate correlations for the Bayley factors reported by Lewis et al. (1986). The Verbal Scale at 12 months had correlations of .22 and .21 for nonadoptive and adoptive pairs, respectively, which suggested no genetic influence but a moderate effect of shared environment. At 24 months, the factors labeled *lexical* and *verbal*, which appear to assess production and comprehension, indicated substantial genetic influence. Finally, Thompson and Plomin (1988) used the Sequenced Inventory of Communication Development to assess language in 2- and 3-year-old adoptees and found both environmental and genetic effects, with the latter effect increasing with age. The variable analyzed by Thompson and Plomin was a combination of expressive and receptive items, but 60% of the items included in the composite were expressive. Thus, the genetic effect on language revealed by adoption studies is primarily an effect on expressive vocabulary and willingness or ability to communicate.

Twin studies are a second tool for exploring genetic effects on language. This method is potentially problematic because twin language is unique in several ways. One aspect of the "twin situation" is that parents direct less speech to individual twins (Bornstein & Ruddy, 1984; Conway, Lytton, & Pysh, 1980; Lytton, Conway, & Sauve, 1977; Stafford, 1987; Tomasello, Mannle, &

Kruger, 1986). A second aspect is that twins often participate in three-way conversations in which they may communicate with either the parent or the co-twin (Savic, 1980). Research comparing twin and nontwin language is sparse, particularly regarding comparisons during the second year for children speaking English. Moreover, when quantitative differences emerge, they often reflect auxiliary processes, such as a tendency to complete each other's utterances (for twins learning Serbo-Croatian, see Savic, 1979), or syntactic or semantic adaptations to twin status, such as misuse of plurals or pronouns (Malmstrom & Silva, 1986).

There is a traditional belief that twin language is developmentally delayed (Day, 1932; McCarthy, 1954), but detailed analysis of twin language reveals some domains in which twins are more advanced than singletons. For example, twins acquire the use of the word *I* relatively quickly (Savic, 1980). Claims that twins have delayed language could arise because twins tend to have low birth weights, but data from the Louisville Twin Study suggest that this difference dissipates over time (Wilson, 1977). Moreover, to the extent that both MZ and DZ twins are at risk for low birth weight, delay would not affect estimates of heritability. Recent research also indicates that twins are prone to phonological disorders that can make their speech less easily intelligible (Dodd & McEvoy, 1994). This could contribute to assertions that twin language is atypical.

The presence of a same-aged sibling certainly alters the linguistic environment, and unique aspects of the twin linguistic environment necessitate some caution in interpreting language data from twins. But these circumstances do not preclude using twins to contrast genetic and environmental effects on language acquisition. In some sense, the twin situation for learning language can be viewed as a special case of the multisibling family context, albeit one in which there is no spacing between two of the siblings.

Twin studies suggest a genetic effect on language in preschool-aged children. Mittler (1969) administered the Illinois Test of Psycholinguistic Abilities to 4-year-old MZ and DZ twins. Subtests that measure expressive language (e.g., the Vocal Encoding subtest, in which the child is asked to describe simple objects, or the Auditory-Vocal Automatic subtest, which measures inflectional aspects of grammar) revealed significant heritable effects. Subtests that should be sensitive to receptive language (e.g., the Auditory Encoding subtest, which assesses the child's ability to understand the spoken word) suggest no heritable effects. Munsinger and Douglass (1976) administered tests of language comprehension and the receptive and expressive use of syntactic forms to twin pairs aged 3.5–17.5 years and found large estimates of heritability for all measures.

Mather and Black (1984) tested preschool twins (mean age = 4.5 years) on standardized measures of vocabulary comprehension, semantic knowledge, morphology, syntax, and articulation[5] and found significant heritability for comprehension and environmental influence for the other measures. However, note that language comprehension skill has a strong relation to measures of general intellectual abilities (e.g., the Peabody Picture Vocabulary Test, used by Mather and Black to measure comprehension, correlates highly with measures of IQ). In a detailed reanalysis of these data, Locke and Mather (1989) discovered that MZ twin pairs were significantly more likely to mispronounce the same sounds on an articulation test than were DZ twin pairs, who in turn shared more errors than children who were unrelated. Finally, Matheny and Bruggemann (1972) used the Templin-Darley Screening Test of Articulation with twins 4–8 years of age and found greater MZ similarity than DZ similarity for boys.

These studies suggest a genetic effect on expressive language in preschool-aged twins, but we know little about genetic and environmental effects on language in the second year, particularly for receptive skills. Leonard, Newhoff, and Mesalam (1980) explored the phonological development of a single set of identical twins from 19 to 22 months. These data suggest some similarities and differences between twins but do not allow a comparison of genetic and environmental effects. Benson, Cherny, Haith, and Fulker (1993) administered the Sequenced Inventory of Communication Development at 5, 7, and 9 months to MZ and DZ twins. They found consistent positive correlations with mid-parent general intelligence (measured using the Wechsler Adult Intelligence Scale–Revised) for the Expressive Scale and less consistent results for the Receptive Scale, but separate MZ and DZ twin correlations were not reported. Cardon and Fulker (1991) reported that a measure of vocalization ability for this sample at 9 months suggested an h^2 of .51 and a c^2 of .38, both statistically significant. Finally, we know of no data that address the presence of genetic and environmental effects on qualitative and quantitative developmental function during the second year or of genetic or environmental contributions to continuity and change across the second year.

[5] For a detailed description of the specific measures, see Mather and Black (1984).

V. NONVERBAL ASPECTS OF INTELLIGENCE

NONVERBAL MDI ITEMS

Many MDI items are nonverbal in the sense that they do not require the ability to speak or to understand language. It is tempting to subdivide this set further: some items require exploration and attention, some require the ability to imitate, and some require that the child understand a means-ends relation. These distinctions have been used to label factor-analytic MDI components described earlier, and they have theoretical relevance within Piagetian and other accounts of cognitive development in the second year. For example, Piaget (1952) suggested that, during the first half of the second year, infants become increasingly sophisticated in their ability to explore objects as entities independent of their own actions. The mechanism of exploration is the tertiary circular reaction in which infants perform systematic variations on actions to see what happens (e.g., hitting objects to hear their sound). Infants are increasingly curious, and they become able to imitate a wide range of unfamiliar actions. These various capacities allow infants to make discoveries about objects and the relations among objects, particularly regarding causality and the means to achieve various ends. The Piagetian account suggests a shift in the latter half of the second year toward the capacity for problem solving through mental representation. This new ability allows infants to infer causes and to assume pretense (e.g., to engage in pretend play).

Unfortunately, the richness of the Piagetian account becomes a drawback if the goal is to subdivide MDI items. Piaget proposed a large set of interconnected processes, and most MDI items tap several of these processes. For example, ringing a bell requires some exploration and attention but is also a means to an end: imitation of a crayon stroke is obviously imitation but also a response to the affordances of crayons and paper. In this *Monograph*, we will adopt the relatively conservative strategy of categorizing all nonverbal MDI items into a single construct. This construct is certainly less specific than the constructs that are formed on the basis of items requiring expressive or receptive language, yet it is more specific than the overarching construct measured by the entire set of MDI items. Within this hierarchy, we will interpret the nonverbal construct as a measure of general cognitive ability, but one different from the MDI in that it is relatively independent of language. Thus, in the appropriate context, the nonverbal items could be administered to (and the nonverbal MDI score could be calculated for) any individual who has appropriate motor ability whether or not that individual speaks a human language.

NONVERBAL TASKS

An alternative approach to identifying aspects of intelligence is to use cognitive tasks that tap specific aspects of intelligence. Procedures that tap such abilities as memory, imitation, or problem solving have the advantages of face validity and specificity, and tasks can be engineered to provide effective and efficient measurement (e.g., Detterman, 1979). Unfortunately, few such procedures have been established for infants in the second year. As noted earlier, this lacuna reflects not only a lack of theoretical interest by researchers but also the difficulty of working with infants in this age range.

One source of guidance for identifying cognitive tasks that could be relevant in the second year is efforts to identify cognitive abilities in infants in the first year that predict intelligence scores in older children. This literature has been reviewed recently by Colombo (1993) and Slater (1994), so an extended presentation is not warranted here. McCall and Carriger's (1993) meta-analytic review of 23 studies in which measures of infant cognition were used to predict later IQ revealed two potent variables: recognition memory (i.e., preferential gaze toward a novel stimulus when it is paired with a previously presented familiar stimulus) and habituation (i.e., a decrement of attention or responsiveness to a repeatedly presented or continuously available stimulus that is not simply the fatigue of sensory receptors). The median correlation between these variables and later IQ was .45, which is all the more impressive within the context of relatively low test-retest reliability for the predictor variables.

The search for early emerging abilities that predict later IQ is relevant to the goals of the present *Monograph*, but two caveats threaten a firm connection. First, McCall and Carriger note that coefficients may be highest for predictions on the basis of assessments between 2 and 8 months of age. In his thematic review, Slater (1994) also concludes that these and other measures that predict later IQ have a temporal window of opportunity during which the measure is predictive. Second, even if we sought to measure these variables, procedures that are effective for assessing cognitive ability in the first year do not necessarily tap the cognitive skills of infants in their second year. Despite

27

differences in age range and the lack of theoretical impetus (particularly in the mid-1980s, when the present study was launched), our search for specific measures of cognitive ability yielded two procedures that bear a strong relation to the measures of recognition memory and habituation that have proved useful in the first year.

Memory for Locations

Recognition memory (i.e., differential response to familiar and novel stimuli) emerges very early in development and is well established before the first birthday. Newborns respond differently to complex auditory stimuli that they heard during the final weeks of gestation (Fifer, 1987), and 3-month-old infants retain knowledge for weeks about a foot-kick contingency that is applicable in a particular context (Rovee-Collier, 1990). As noted earlier, investigations indicate that individual differences in infant recognition memory assessed during the middle of the first year may capture a dimension of information processing that significantly affects subsequent cognitive ability (Colombo, 1993; McCall & Carriger, 1993; Slater, 1994), but the efficacy of this prediction abates before the first birthday. Thus, recognition memory did not seem useful as a dimension of individual differences in the second year.

Recall memory, in which a memory trace is reexperienced spontaneously or arises because of some cue or probe, emerges later in the first year. For example, Diamond and Doar (1989) used a delayed-response task requiring infants to recall the location of a hidden toy and found that 8-month-olds fail to reach to the correct location if any delay is imposed between hiding and finding but that 12-month-olds can bridge an 8-second delay. When the test is made more challenging by expanding the number of locations, there is systematic improvement in recall memory for locations from 1 to 3 years (Fox, Kagan, & Weiskopf, 1979; Kagan, 1981; Kagan & Hamburg, 1981; Kagan, Kearsley, & Zelazo, 1978). The memory for locations task taps a short-term storage process that seems different from recognition memory but that is relevant in the second year and is a component of many theories of adult information processing (e.g., Atkinson & Shiffrin, 1968; Broadbent, 1958; Cowan, 1988). It is interesting to note that the memory for locations task requires not only memory but also the inhibition of prepotent responses (Diamond, 1990; Hofstadter & Reznick, 1996). McCall (1994) has speculated that the infant's ability to inhibit looking at the familiar stimulus may be the underlying mechanism that unites recognition memory and habituation and that supports the relation between these constructs and later IQ.

Kagan (1981) has mapped changes in memory for location ability during the second year for infants in the United States and in Fiji, and these curves suggest an asymptote at about 2 years. We do not know whether individual differences in memory for locations are preserved or the relative effect of genetic and environmental influences.

Attention to Visual Stimuli

The tendency to orient toward different aspects of the environment plays a complex and significant role in theoretical accounts of cognitive development. Posner and Petersen (1990) delineate three subsystems that have been prominent in cognitive accounts of attention: (*a*) orienting to sensory events (e.g., foveating a stimulus); (*b*) detecting signals for conscious processing (e.g., monitoring a stream of auditory information for a word); and (*c*) maintaining a vigilant or alert state (e.g., preparing to respond when a stimulus appears at a particular location). Ruff and Rothbart (1996) offer a similar taxonomy: attention as selector, as state, and as executive control. Moreover, the fact that the child attends to discrepant, salient, or novel targets suggests that attentiveness reflects not only the detection of information but also the ongoing processing of that information and the status of the relation between the new information and the child's existing knowledge. In some circumstances, enhanced attention suggests more sophisticated processing, as when an infant notices a subtle discrepancy or engages in the assimilation of a new stimulus. In other circumstances, enhanced attention is less impressive, as when an infant's enhanced attention reflects a failure to notice that a stimulus is being repeated (i.e., the infant is slow to habituate) or a failure to assimilate a new stimulus.

Attentiveness in children has been measured in various ways: as visual or manual orientation to stimuli; as sustained response to a single stimulus or sequence of unique stimuli; and in situations where stimulus access is controlled by the experimenter or by the child. Given this range of operational definitions and, as noted earlier, the range of interpretations for any act of sustained attention, a definitive assessment of attentiveness would require a comprehensive battery of tests, evoking various responses across a range of stimulus materials. In the present study, we measured attentiveness as the duration of gaze to visual stimuli, which taps the infant's detection of signals for cognitive processing and desire to assimilate a new stimulus. Thus, attentiveness as measured here is similar to the construct that Ruff and Rothbart (1996) call *focused attention* and define as the ability to become narrowly selective when necessary or appropriate and to redirect energy and resources to the selected activity. Visual attentiveness should increase with age as long as the stimuli are interesting, are presented briefly, and appear in a context that evokes the child's desire to process the stimuli. A comparable positive relation between age and attention has been demonstrated for duration of

29

engagement with toys (e.g., Kopp & Vaughn, 1982; Sigman, Cohen, Beckwith, & Topinka, 1987).

Colombo (1993) and Ruff (1990) reviewed the extensive literature on individual differences in attentiveness in infants and toddlers and found evidence for short-term and long-term stability, but the relative influence of heredity and environment is unclear. Ruff and Rothbart (1996) report evidence suggesting short-term stability and some tendency toward long-term stability in focused attention. Neural mechanisms have been identified that may account for individual differences (Colombo, 1995), but these mechanisms could be influenced by genetic or environmental effects. The role of genetic mediation of attentiveness has been addressed using observer report. Matheny (1980, 1983) factor analyzed the Bayley Infant Behavior Record and found a coherent cluster among items in which the observer noted the child's tendency to remain attentive, responsive, and goal directed during administration of the BSID. Twin data from the Louisville Twin Study indicated that this construct, labeled *task orientation,* was significantly heritable at 12, 18, and 24 months. Braungart, Plomin, DeFries, and Fulker (1992) replicated this effect in an analysis of sibling adoption data and twin data and reported heritability at 12 and 24 months of .40 and .47, respectively.

VI. THE PRESENT STUDY

The MacArthur Longitudinal Twin Study is an ongoing behavioral genetic investigation of cognitive, social, emotional, and temperamental aspects of behavior being conducted at the Institute for Behavioral Genetics at the University of Colorado. Same-sex twin pairs were observed at 14, 20, and 24 months using an extensive battery described elsewhere (for details, see Plomin, Campos, et al., 1990). Additional assessment of this cohort at older ages is under way.

BIRTH WEIGHT

The intrauterine growth of singletons and twins tends to be parallel until about 34 weeks of gestation (Naeye, Benirschke, Hagstrom, & Marcus, 1966) but then slows for twins, resulting in many twins being born light and small for gestational age (MacGillivray, Nylander, & Corney, 1975; Merenstein, Kaplan, & Rosenberg, 1991; Nichols & Broman, 1974). Low birth weight is a major correlate of infant mortality and childhood morbidity, and the effects of low birth weight are well documented.[6] To reduce the effect of birth weight, twins in the present sample were selected to be relatively heavy. This constraint affects comparability with twin studies that do not screen for birth weight, but it increases our confidence in generalizations from the present sample to a broad range of normally developing children.

ASSESSMENT AGES

The decision to assess at 14, 20, and 24 months, rather than at symmetrical intervals (e.g., 12, 18, and 24 months), warrants comment. Equally spaced intervals would have allowed symmetry in descriptions of changes in develop-

---

[6] For a summary of recent reports, see, e.g., Shiono and Behrman (1995).

mental function and would have supported inferences about the absolute magnitude of change during the first half and second half of the second year. However, previous research and theory (e.g., Fischer, 1980; McCall et al., 1977; Piaget, 1952; Uzgiris, 1976) have already provided some insight into cognitive development during this time period, and these studies suggest that there are significant transitions, inflections, or qualitative shifts in performance at about the first birthday and in the latter half of the second year. The 12–13 month transition was not a major focus in the present work, so the first assessment was conducted shortly thereafter, at 14 months. Transition late in the second year was of particular interest in the present study, so the second assessment was conducted at 20 months to be more proximal to that age range. The final assessment was conducted 4 months later, to bracket change late in the second year.

DEPENDENT VARIABLES

Intelligence

The Mental Scale of the BSID was administered, and the MDI was calculated according to standardized procedures. However, as noted earlier, for some analyses the items on the MDI were divided into three theoretically defined constructs: *expressive language, receptive language,* and *nonverbal items.*

Language

Language was assessed directly using an abbreviated version of the Sequenced Inventory of Communication Development (SICD; Hedrick, Prather, & Tobin, 1975). This standardized assessment of general communicative performance has separate tests of expressive and receptive language skills and combines observer report with parent report. To provide a more objective measurement of comprehension vocabulary, children were also tested on a cued-target procedure in which comprehension ability was inferred from behavior. Specifically, children saw pairs of slides of objects, and their fixations to the slides were recorded. After an initial salience assessment phase, the children were cued with a verbal label for one of the objects. Comprehension was inferred from an increase in fixation to the named object. Researchers have used this technique to explore various aspects of receptive language ability and have discovered improvement in word comprehension from 8 to 20 months and acceptable reliability and validity (Golinkoff, Hirsh-Pasek, Cauley, & Gordon, 1987; Hirsh-Pasek, Golinkoff, Fletcher, deGaspe Beaubien, & Cauley, 1985; Naigles, 1990; Naigles & Gelman, 1995; Reznick,

1982, 1990; Reznick & Goldfield, 1992; Thomas, Campos, Shucard, Ramsey, & Shucard, 1981).

Memory for Locations

Recall memory was assessed by using a memory for locations test derived from the delayed-response procedure reported by Hunter (1913) but more familiar to developmentalists as Piaget's test for object permanence (Piaget, 1952; Uzgiris & Hunt, 1975). Kagan and his colleagues have developed a systematic protocol within the delayed-response task to study the child's search for hidden objects under increasing task difficulty defined by varying the number of hiding sites and the length of delay between hiding and search (Kagan, 1981). Higher scores imply the ability to retain and act on information about the location of a hidden object despite interference from other possible responses and the decay of memory across time.

Visual Attentiveness

We were not able to administer tasks of visual attentiveness per se but used a peripheral measurement to tap one aspect of this ability. In the word-comprehension procedure described earlier, children saw a series of pairs of slides of objects. Attentiveness was measured as the average duration of gaze to these stimuli during the noncued phase (i.e., before the experimenter cued the child with a label for one of the slides). Note that the present task does not require the extended monitoring of specific targets that is the hallmark of traditional sustained attention tasks (Davies, Jones, & Taylor, 1984; Warm, 1984). Thus, we are probably not tapping the infant's increasing speed at assimilating novel stimuli, which causes fixation duration to drop dramatically during the first year (Colombo, 1993; Colombo & Mitchell, 1990). It is possible that some infants who are not interested in the naming game will be affected by a tendency to assimilate quickly and then look away, but this trend could be identified by the presence of a bimodal distribution of looking times.

RELATION TO PREVIOUS REPORTS OF THE MACARTHUR LONGITUDINAL TWIN STUDY

Earlier reports have examined a broad array of variables for subsets of the MacArthur cohort cross-sectionally at 14 months (Emde et al., 1992; Plomin, Campos, et al., 1990) and longitudinally at 14 and 20 months (Plomin et al., 1993). Other reports have focused on the domains of temperament or emotion (e.g., Cherny, Fulker, Corley, et al., 1994; DiLalla, Kagan, & Reznick, 1994; Robinson, Kagan, Reznick, & Corley, 1992; Robinson, Zahn-Waxler, & Emde, 1994; Zahn-Waxler, Robinson, & Emde, 1992) or on a single measure of intellectual behavior (e.g., Cherny, Fulker, Emde, et al., 1994). The present study extends these analyses to include measurements at 24 months, expands the sample to include the entire cohort that was tested in this age range, and establishes constructs for analysis that reflect general cognitive ability as well as specific aspects of cognitive ability. The relation between the present results and the findings from previous reports of data from this cohort will be described below.[7]

[7] Some previous reports of the MacArthur Longitudinal Twin Study mention a sorting/categorization variable. This variable was assessed at only 14 and 20 months and will therefore not be included here.

VII. METHOD

Four hundred eight same-sex twin pairs (equally distributed by sex) were recruited from monthly reports of births from the Colorado Department of Health. Twins were selected preferentially for higher birth weight (1,700 grams or more) and normal gestational age (34 weeks or more), but some healthy small infants were included. The average birth weight for the sample was 2,579 grams (SD = 469). Birth weights were normally distributed and ranged between 1,191 and 4,763 grams. Only 4% of the infants weighed less than 1,700 grams at birth. The median gap between the births of the two twins was 3 minutes; 90% of births were within 35 minutes of each other. Secondborn twins had lower Apgar scores ($F[1, 804] = 7.86$, $p < .01$) but did not differ on birth weight or on any of the outcome variables that will be described subsequently (cf. Bornstein & Ruddy, 1984).

Eligible families were invited to participate via a letter, and over 50% accepted. The ethnic distribution of the 408 participating families was 88.5% European-American, 9% Hispanic-American, and 2.5% African-American. The vast majority were two-parent families with both parents somewhat older than the average Colorado parents of newborns (30 years vs. 28 years) and having more education (14.3 years vs. 12.5 years). The distribution of educational accomplishment for mothers was as follows: 8% had not graduated from high school, 25% had no education beyond high school, 49% had attended some college, and 17% had some education beyond college. Fathers had slightly more education than mothers, but the distribution of accomplishment was almost identical: 6% had not graduated from high school, 28% had no education beyond high school, 49% had attended some college, and 17% had some education beyond college. Within a family, mothers and fathers had highly similar educational attainment ($r[395] = .62$, $p < .01$). The median difference between education for mothers and fathers was 1 year, with 59% of families reporting no difference or a difference of 1 year. Intelligence scores available for a subset of 178 parents were correlated .51. These cross-parent similarities in education and intelligence suggest a marked tendency toward assortative mating. As will be noted later, similarity between spouses who are the parents of DZ twins tends to diminish estimates of genetic effects by reducing the MZ-DZ twin difference.

Families were tested three times in the laboratory and three times in their homes. The first home visit occurred between 13.5 and 15.5 months, the second between 19.5 and 21.5 months, and the third between 23.5 and 26.5 months. Laboratory visits occurred within this same interval, usually 1–2 weeks after the home visit. The age span at each assessment point was relatively wide, reflecting the difficulty of enforcing timely appointments for infants, a difficulty exacerbated by the vagaries of Colorado weather and the logistic problems that arise for families with twins. Despite these difficulties, the age distributions for each assessment point were leptokurtic, with median assessment ages of 14.2 months and 14.6 months for home and laboratory, respectively, at 14 months, 20.2 and 20.6 months for home and laboratory at 20 months, and 24.3 and 24.8 months for home and laboratory at 24 months. Each distribution had some positive skew because upward limits were stretched in an effort to reduce the amount of missing data.

HOME VISIT PROCEDURES

Two female examiners visited each home. Examiners were blind to any previous data except, as will be noted later, when language testing began with an item that had been failed on the previous visit. Examiners were not blind to zygosity to the extent that zygosity was determined on the basis of examiner ratings of the twin pair's physical similarity (as will be described later) and was often obvious for DZ twins. However, each examiner was blind to the ratings of zygosity provided by other examiners and to the final zygosity determination, which was defined on the basis of average agreement across raters.

The relatively long test battery (described in full by Emde et al., 1992) and the need to complete all testing in a single visit necessitated that the cognitive test be administered to the twins simultaneously. To accomplish this, the examiners worked independently in separate rooms with the twin seated in a high chair. In most cases, the mother hovered in the doorway in sight of both twins. In the few cases in which a twin refused to cooperate, the mother held that twin on her lap. If both twins refused to cooperate, the examiners rescheduled the home visit and returned on a subsequent day.

Testing at home, and particularly testing twins simultaneously, does not reflect ideal standardized testing conditions. The disadvantage of this testing context is that it may have introduced unnecessary error variance in test scores. However, we deemed this disadvantage warranted when offset by the advantage of testing twins in a familiar environment and not after a long drive to a laboratory appointment. Moreover, travel with young twins is difficult at best for most parents, so some home visit testing was necessary to obtain the quantity of data needed and maintain the allegiance of parents in this longitudinal study.

On the initial home visit, examiners were randomly assigned to each twin. On subsequent visits to the same home, the examiner was assigned to the twin whom she had not previously tested. At 20 and 24 months, testers were blind to each twin's previous performance except for the SICD, for which previous test results were used to determine the first item to be administered.

Bayley Scales of Infant Development

The mental development component of the BSID (Bayley, 1969) was administered with the child seated in a high chair, but a few children sat in a booster seat or in their mother's lap. The test was administered according to standardized procedures, with basal and ceiling levels established to derive the MDI.

As noted earlier, we used a strategy adopted by Kohen-Raz (1967) and Dale et al. (1989) to sort items on the BSID that are typically administered in the second year into subsets with theoretical coherence. Two sets of inherently linguistic items were identified: items that require expressive language skills (e.g., naming objects) and items that require receptive language skills (e.g., pointing to named pictures). Items that required ambiguous language skills (e.g., items that required both expressive and receptive language or that assessed imitation using a linguistic response) were excluded from further analysis. The remaining items (e.g., ringing a bell, attaining a toy with a stick) were combined into a set that was considered nonverbal. Items that had verbal instructions but that could have been solved without comprehension of the instructions (e.g., the experimenter gives the child a broken doll and asks him or her to put it together) were considered nonverbal. Appendix A lists the BSID items retained for the components (i.e., *only* those items that met the criteria for inclusion stated earlier) and the percentage of subjects passing each item at each age.

One strategy for assessing the validity of our assignment of items into categories is to compare our designations with the categories used by others. Kohen-Raz (1967) used an earlier version of the BSID. Despite some differences in the content of specific items, every BSID item that we considered to be expressive is categorized by Kohen-Raz as relevant for the Vocalization Scale, and all age-relevant items on the Kohen-Raz Vocalization Scale were included in our set of expressive items. For receptive items, all BSID items that we considered receptive and that were available to Kohen-Raz were classified as *comprehension*. However, because Kohen-Raz included imitation items in the same category as comprehension, the Kohen-Raz scale contained some items that we did not use. As noted earlier, we considered verbal imitation items to be ambiguous and excluded them. The items that we categorized as nonverbal were further divided by Kohen-Raz into *eye-hand, manipulation,* and *object relation,* but we did not have sufficient confidence in the theoretical coherence of these subsets of items.

We compared our categorization of items with the sets reported by Dale et al. (1989). The only differences were because of items noted earlier, which we deleted as ambiguous, and items with verbal instructions that could have been solved without comprehension of the instructions, which we considered nonverbal. We compared our categorization with the factors identified by Lewis et al. (1986). Their 12-month factor, labeled *verbal-skill,* contained only three items, two of which were in our expressive category. At 24 months, 18 of 24 items labeled *lexical* or *verbal symbolic* were in our expressive or receptive categories, but the distinction between the two Lewis et al. linguistic categories was not obvious and did not correspond to our a priori distinction between expressive and receptive language. Finally, we compared our categorization of items with the designation of facets in the recent revision of the BSID (Bayley, 1993). Some items that we administered have been deleted from the BSID-2, but, for the items that have been retained, there was complete overlap between our designation of expressive or receptive language and the BSID-2 designation of relevance for the "language facet."

Sequenced Inventory of Communication Development

Items from the expressive and receptive components of the SICD (Hedrick et al., 1975) were administered concurrently with the BSID to take advantage of the significant overlap between the two measures. SICD items derived from parent report were gathered at the end of the home visit. We used the subset of items designated for children several months above and below the target age rather than a complete SICD to reduce the length of the procedure. The disadvantage of this decision is that our SICD scoring system is ad hoc, but the advantage is that each child's performance is more likely to be optimal.

For the SICD Expressive Scale at 14 months, items 9–20 and 22–26 were administered. At each subsequent visit, we began testing with items the child had failed at earlier ages and added age-relevant items: items 27PR, 28, 29PR, and 30a were added at 20 months, and items 29a, 29b, 30d, 31a, and 32 were added at 24 months. The same strategy of item selection was used for the

SICD Receptive Scale at 14 months: items 6–18 were administered at 14 months, items 19a and 20a were added at 20 months, and items 21a–21c, 22PR, 23, and 24a–24c were added at 24 months.[8]

LABORATORY PROCEDURES

Cognitive tests were administered to each twin separately with the mother present. A single examiner tested both twins but was not aware of any relevant data. As noted earlier, the zygosity of most DZ twins was self-evident, but the examiner was not aware of any prior zygosity ratings.

Word Comprehension

The child sat in a high chair, 27 inches from two rear-projection screens placed side by side, 9 inches apart. The mother was seated next to the child or, in rare cases, held the child on her lap. Mothers who held their child were asked to avoid altering the child's posture in a way that might influence response toward either screen. The experimenter monitored compliance with this request and repeated it if necessary. The experimenter watched through a small window above the screen and pushed a toggle switch to indicate the child's visual fixation to the slide on the left or right. The experimenter was unaware of the identity of the slides. A computer cumulated the fixation to each slide on each trial.

Each word-comprehension trial had two phases. In the preprompt phase, a pair of slides, each depicting a different object, was visible for 8 seconds while the experimenter recorded fixation to the slides. The slides went off for 1 second and then reappeared in exactly the same locations. The experimenter, who was visible through an opening above the slides but blind to the location of specific slides, then asked the child, "Do you see the ———? Where is the ———? Look at the ———," substituting a word that named one of the slides. The slides remained visible for 8 seconds while the experimenter prompted the child and recorded fixation. Following a 3-second intertrial interval, the procedure was repeated with another slide pair and another word prompt.

Each child saw 15 word-comprehension pairs composed of words selected to be either easy, moderately difficult, or extremely difficult to comprehend (on the basis of norms available from early versions of the MacArthur Communicative Development Inventories; for details, see Fenson et al., 1993). The presentation was ordered in such a way that each block of three

[8] An item with a particular number on the SICD Expressive Scale is not related to the item with that same number on the Receptive Scale.

words contained one word from each level of difficulty. The words tested at 14 months were *ball, balloon, bee, blocks, boat, bread, broom, car, cat, dog, lamp, purse, shoe, socks,* and *tree.* At 20 months, the words were *bike, cake, camera, crib, drawer, elephant, fork, frog, hand, jacket, map, mop, pencil, penguin,* and *pillow.* At 24 months, the words were *alligator, birdhouse, cowboy, flag, glove, jar, ladder, refrigerator, roof, scarf, slipper, snowman, wolf,* and *zebra.* The pictures in each pair were balanced for salience along several dimensions, including size, color, and complexity.

Memory for Locations

The child sat in a high chair at a small table, across from and facing an experimenter. In a few cases, the child sat in the mother's lap. Two 2-ounce plastic cups were placed on a $24 \times 5\frac{3}{4}$-inch board in inverted positions $1\frac{1}{2}$ inches apart and centered in front of the child. The experimenter allowed the child to play with a small, attractive toy and then placed it under one of the inverted cups. She then held an 8×24-inch sheet of masonite between the child and the cups to block the child's view of the cups and impose a brief delay interval. After this interval, the shield was removed, and the child was encouraged to find the toy. A correct response was coded if the child removed the appropriate cup. If the child removed both cups, the trial was repeated.

Each memory for locations test session began with a brief series of warm-up trials with two cups at 0 seconds (i.e., no occlusion) until the child demonstrated comprehension of the task by finding the hidden toy. The first test trial contained two cups at a 1-second occlusion. The number of cups and the delay interval were changed on succeeding trials on the basis of the child's response pattern. Correct trials with two cups at the 1-second delay were followed by trials with 5-second and 10-second delays. Correct response at the 10-second delay led to an increase from two to four cups (or from four to six cups) but a return to the 1-second delay. Correct performance on six cups at the 10-second delay led to a final trial at a 15-second delay, presumed to be above ceiling for most children in this age range. If a child was incorrect at any level, that level was repeated once. A second failure ended the procedure.

ZYGOSITY

Zygosity of the twins was determined through aggregation of independent tester ratings on the similarity of ten physical attributes across age. The attributes were selected on the basis of the diagnostic rules developed by Nichols and Bilbro (1966). If the features of the pair of twins were rated consistently as highly similar (i.e., scores of 1 or 2 on a five-point scale), the classification MZ was made. If two or more features were only somewhat similar (i.e., a score of 3), or if one feature was not at all similar (i.e., score of 4 or 5), the classification DZ was made. Zygosity of twin pairs was rated at five age points currently assessed in this longitudinal study (namely, 14, 24, 36, 48, and 60 months); for a few twin pairs, zygosity was also assessed at 20 months. At 14, 20, 24, and 36 months, twin zygosity was independently rated by two home and two laboratory testers. The two home testers rated zygosity at later age points. In the present analysis, the modal number of zygosity ratings per subject was 18. Twin zygosity was considered unambiguous if there was 85% agreement of the MZ or DZ classification across all testers at all ages, on the basis of a minimum of four ratings. A subset of the twin pairs with ambiguous ratings had their zygosity determined through an evaluation of genetic markers from blood samples: seven were classified as MZ and two as DZ. The current zygosity distribution for the 408 families is 210 MZ pairs, 177 DZ pairs, and 21 unresolved ambiguous pairs.

SUBJECT ATTRITION

The sample consists of 408 twin pairs who were tested in the home or the laboratory at 14, 20, or 24 months; 252 of these twin pairs participated in both the home and the laboratory at all three ages. A few families discontinued participation because of change of residence, employment demands, or lack of commitment to the project. Because the laboratory visit entailed a significant automobile trip and was required within a narrow window of weeks, the most frequent pattern of missing data was the 17% of twin pairs who were unable to attend one or more laboratory visits. The second most frequent pattern of missing data was the 13% of twin pairs who missed one or more age assessments (i.e., both the home and the laboratory visit) because of illness, weather, or general difficulty in scheduling.

To make the best use of the data, each analysis was calculated using all the twin pairs that were available for that particular analysis. That is, cross-sectional analyses at 14 months were based on 395 twin pairs for home visits and 342 pairs for laboratory visits; analyses at 20 months were based on 354 twin pairs for home visits and 300 pairs for laboratory visits; and analyses at 24 months were based on 354 twin pairs for home visits and 321 pairs for laboratory visits. The strategy of including all available data created some confusion in that the sample size changed across analyses, but this inconvenience was offset by the boost in statistical power afforded by not limiting the sample

41

to the 252 twin pairs with data from each assessment at 14, 20, and 24 months. For most analyses, we compared results for the entire cohort with results for two subsets of subjects with no missing data: one subset contained subjects who had complete data for the relevant measure at all three ages; the second contained the 252 twin pairs who participated in the home and laboratory assessments at all three ages. Any discrepancies between the primary analysis and either of these two additional analyses are noted.

VIII. CALCULATION OF VARIABLES

We present results from this large and complex data set in six separate chapters. In the present chapter, we describe the procedures for calculating each dependent variable and provide evidence for reliability and validity. In the chapter that follows, we focus on the relation among dependent variables. This will include intercorrelations and also a description of qualitative developmental function (i.e., age-related changes in the behaviors that are most salient or prominent for an individual infant). In Chapter X, we report analyses of group differences. These analyses include effects of age, sex, and zygosity and also a description of quantitative developmental function (i.e., patterns of age-related change). Our focus in Chapter XI is on individual differences. Various influences are explored, including effects of birth weight, assessment age, parents' education, and physical similarity. We then report the stability of individual differences over time, using cross-time correlations and within-subject comparisons of quantitative developmental function. In Chapter XII, we report extensive analyses of genetic and environmental effects, and, in Chapter XIII, we provide a brief summary of the entire set of results.

PRELIMINARY INVESTIGATION OF SICD ITEMS

SICD items were either expressive or receptive and were derived from either observation or parent report. Percentage correct scores calculated across items in each of these four categories or for combinations of categories (i.e., expressive vs. receptive, parent report vs. observation) were significantly intercorrelated at each age, with coefficients ranging between .20 and .57. However, there were marked differences in *twin resemblance* for percentage correct scores derived from observation in comparison to percentage correct scores derived from parent-report items. As indicated in Table 1, intraclass twin correlations for MZ and DZ twins on percentage correct for both the Receptive and the Expressive Scales were markedly higher for parent-report

TABLE 1

<small>Intraclass Twin Correlations on Percentage Correct for SICD Expressive and Receptive Items Separated into Parent Report and Observer Report</small>

	MZ Twins			DZ Twins		
Age and Items	Parent	Observer	z	Parent	Observer	z
14 months:						
Expressive	.80	.31	7.78**	.70	.26	6.01**
	(203)	(202)		(171)	(170)	
Receptive	.91	.60	8.37**	.90	.47	9.60**
	(203)	(203)		(170)	(170)	
20 months:						
Expressive	.82	.65	3.85**	.77	.46	5.53**
	(179)	(177)		(156)	(154)	
Receptive	.78	.64	2.87**	.79	.55	4.53**
	(179)	(179)		(156)	(156)	
24 months:						
Expressive	.82	.79	.86	.75	.54	3.69**
	(174)	(174)		(155)	(153)	
Receptive	.92	.68	7.78**	.85	.53	6.66**
	(174)	(174)		(155)	(155)	

<small>Note.—Degrees of freedom are given in parentheses. All correlations in this table are statistically significant at $p <$ .01. The differences between parent report and observer report correlations are expressed in one-tailed z scores.
** $p < .01$.</small>

items than for observer-report items for almost every comparison. The difference between correlations was statistically significant for 11 of 12 comparisons (z scores are listed in Table 1); parent-report versus observer-report differences tended to be larger for younger infants.

The difference in twin resemblance measured by parent report and by observation is disturbing, and it is important to determine which source is more reliable. Parents are generally good observers of child language and are able to report the language accomplishments for the twinship, but these results suggest that parents may fail to differentiate the language accomplishments of their twins. To avoid this potential source of error, we adopted the conservative strategy of not including SICD items derived from parent report in the expressive and receptive language constructs.[9] The resulting construct may reflect a limited range of the child's linguistic ability, but, given that each member of a twin pair was tested by a different examiner, any twin similarity that emerges for this construct should be relatively reliable.

[9] In questions 79, 89, and 113 of the BSID, the parent is asked about the child's expressive or receptive abilities, but as a guide for the experimenter's probes. A correct response is not credited unless the experimenter hears the child express the particular syllable or word.

EXPRESSIVE LANGUAGE CONSTRUCT

The SICD is designed to measure communication rather than language per se. Thus, the Expressive Scale of the SICD includes assessment of communicative behaviors pertaining to initiation, imitation, and verbal response. Items to assess initiation were all derived from parent report and were therefore excluded. Preliminary analysis of the subsets of imitation and verbal response items revealed a strong correlation between them, but the constructs being measured by each subset seemed to be markedly different. To maintain conceptual clarity, items pertaining to imitation were excluded, with the result that the expressive construct was a measure of explicitly expressive abilities: verbal response, spontaneous speech, and naming. Appendix A lists the SICD items *retained* for the expressive construct (i.e., items that measure expressive ability and that do not rely on parent report) and the percentage of subjects passing each item at each age. Appendix A also lists the BSID items that pertained to expressive language.

Administration procedures for the BSID and the SICD dictated that each infant be tested on items that spanned his or her range of competence. Thus, all infants were tested on some expressive items, but no infant was tested on all expressive items. To calculate an expressive language score, we accepted the logic of the administration procedure and assumed that each infant would have passed the items on that construct that were not administered because they were too easy and would have failed the items on that construct that were not administered because they were too hard. These assumptions raise some questions but must be accepted because of practical constraints on testing young children. A child who is required to respond to a large set of nonchallenging items will become fatigued, and a child who is required to respond to a large set of overly challenging items will become frustrated. In either case, performance will deteriorate. The strategy used in this study establishes a balance between the quality and the quantity of measurement for each child.

To form an expressive language construct, relevant items on the BSID or the SICD for which children's responses were either 100% or 0% correct at a particular age were eliminated, and percentage correct was calculated across the remaining items. Cronbach's alphas (Cronbach, 1951) for the final set of 12, 14, and 16 items in the expressive construct were .64, .87, and .88 at 14, 20, and 24 months, respectively, indicating strong internal consistency.

As noted earlier, parent report may provide a questionable estimate of twin resemblance, but it has the advantage of the parent's opportunity for extensive observation in a variety of contexts. Therefore, although parent report was deemed inadequate to measure the language ability of *individual twins,* mid-twin scores (i.e., the average of the two twins' parent-reported scores) are a useful estimate of the language development of *the twinship* and provide an opportunity to assess the general validity of the expressive language construct. An index of parent-reported expressive language was formed by computing a percentage correct score for each twin across parent-report items on the SICD (items 15a–15c, 16, 17, 18, 20, 27, 28, and 29) and then averaging the scores for the two twins in each family. This score was significantly correlated with a mid-twin expressive language score calculated as the percentage correct for observer-reported expressive items on the BSID and SICD across the two twins in each family ($r[397] = .40$, $p < .01$, $r[355] = .50$, $p < .01$, and $r[354] = .56$, $p < .01$, at 14, 20, and 24 months, respectively). Separate correlations for MZ and DZ twins were comparable. These correlations between parents and observers are modest, accounting for only 16%– 31% of the overlap in variance, but suggest that, to some extent, parents and observers are both tapping related sorts of language abilities. This positive relation bolsters confidence in the validity of the expressive language construct.

RECEPTIVE LANGUAGE CONSTRUCT

The SICD Receptive Scale includes items designed to measure the child's awareness, discrimination, and understanding of language. To meet the goals of this study, items were retained that measured the child's understanding of single- or multiword utterances. Appendix A lists the items from the SICD Receptive Scale that met criteria for inclusion in the receptive language construct. These items were combined with comparable items from the BSID (also listed in Appendix A) to form a construct representing receptive language. As noted earlier, items not administered because they were likely to be too easy were counted as correct, and items not administered because they were likely to be too difficult were counted as incorrect. Items for which children's responses were either 100% or 0% correct at a particular age were eliminated, and a percentage correct score was calculated across the remaining items. Cronbach's alphas for the 30, 37, and 40 items in each set were .79, .89, and .86 at 14, 20, and 24 months, respectively—acceptably high and comparable to alphas for the expressive construct.

Mid-twin scores were calculated for parent-report items on the SICD Receptive Scale and were compared with the percentage correct scores across observed receptive items on the BSID and the SICD. The correlations were $r(397) = .53$, $p < .01$, $r(355) = .65$, $p < .01$, and $r(355) = .53$, $p < .01$, at 14, 20, and 24 months, respectively. Separate correlations for MZ and DZ twins were of comparable magnitude. As noted earlier for expressive language, the overlapping variance is low (only 28%–42%), but the positive relation suggests that parents and observers seem to be tapping related sorts of language abilities.

NONVERBAL CONSTRUCT

MDI items that required neither expressive nor receptive language were combined to form a nonverbal construct. These items are listed in Appendix A. Items not administered because they were too easy were counted as correct; items that were not administered because they were too hard were counted as incorrect. Items for which children's responses were either 100% or 0% correct were eliminated. Cronbach's alphas for the remaining 49, 43, and 32 items were .80, .82, and .82 at 14, 20, and 24 months, respectively, indicating acceptable statistical coherence for the nonverbal construct. Percentage correct was calculated across the nonverbal items. Inspection of the items suggests that the nonverbal construct reflects the child's development of fine motor coordination, the ability to imitate, and the ability to use a means-end strategy to solve simple problems. As noted earlier, we interpreted the nonverbal construct as a measure of general cognitive development that is not dependent on language.

WORD COMPREHENSION

Inspection of the data revealed some word-comprehension trials on which performance was ambiguous because the infant had not fixated both stimuli. Fixation to just one stimulus could indicate a marked preference for that stimulus, but not necessarily relative to the other stimulus. A conservative criterion was adopted in which word-comprehension trials were eliminated if fixation to either side before the word prompt was 0 seconds or if fixation to both sides after the word prompt was 0 seconds. This caused the loss of 20%, 15%, and 11% of trials at 14, 20, and 24 months, respectively.

Percentage fixation to the target slide before the experimenter's prompt for that target was subtracted from percentage fixation to the target slide after the prompt. This calculation indicated whether the child showed an increase in fixation to the target relative to its initial salience. Following the guidelines established in previous research (Reznick, 1990; Reznick & Goldfield, 1992), an increase of 15% was accepted as the criterion indicating comprehension of each word.[10] A word-comprehension score was created by dividing the number of words comprehended by the number of word tests available. The modal denominator for this ratio was 15, but the denominator was lower for some children because of exclusion for low fixation (described

[10] Under this criterion, target slides that attracted 85% or more fixation before the word prompt could not possibly be comprehended. This situation occurred rarely (on fewer than 5% of trials). We conducted additional analyses in which we set these trials to missing, but this did not affect the pattern of significant effects.

earlier) or because of refusal to participate. Word-comprehension scores derived from three or fewer trials were considered unreliable and were therefore treated as missing. This constraint eliminated word-comprehension data for 2.5%, 1.2%, and 1.2% of children at 14, 20, and 24 months, respectively. The correlations between number of word-comprehension trials available and word-comprehension score were low at each age (r = .03, .10, and .08, respectively). Some children may have been inattentive because they did not understand the words, but, in general, comprehension ability per se did not affect the child's willingness to participate in the procedure.

A pilot study was conducted with a small sample of singletons from a comparable population (15 children at 14 months and 16 children at 20 months) to assess the reliability of the word-comprehension scores. Each child was tested on the word-comprehension procedure twice, with a 2-week test-retest interval. The same 15 words were assessed in the same order each time, but the left-right position of the slides was reversed. The procedure was identical to the procedure used in this study. Word-comprehension scores for test and retest were significantly correlated ($r[29]$ = .52, $p < .01$). This level of test-retest reliability is relatively low, but it may have been deflated by a residual lack of interest that accompanied the second presentation of the word-comprehension trials.

The word-comprehension procedure was developed recently; thus, its validity is not well established. We assessed predictive validity for the word-comprehension scores by comparing the average comprehension score for each word, which can be interpreted as the percentage of children who comprehended that word, with norms from the MacArthur Communicative Development Inventories (CDI; Fenson et al., 1993), in which 1,813 parents of children aged 8–30 months completed checklists to indicate the words their child comprehends or produces. All but three of the words tested here were available in the CDI norms. The comprehension scores from this study and the scores for these same words in the CDI norms were significantly correlated ($r[40]$ = .70, $p < .01$). This comparison was derived from CDI norms for production only, but it is reasonable to expect that the number of children comprehending and producing each word should be related. The CDI norms contain parent report of comprehension at 14 months. The word-comprehension score measured here and the CDI normative comprehension score at 14 months were significantly correlated ($r[12]$ = .81, $p < .01$).

VISUAL ATTENTIVENESS

A score reflecting visual attentiveness was calculated on the basis of visual fixation during the word-comprehension procedure. Specifically, the duration of visual fixation to either slide across the preprompt phase of the word-comprehension test was averaged across the 15 trials. The distribution of visual attentiveness scores was negatively skewed at each age but clearly unimodal. This suggests that the visual attentiveness score measures engagement in the ongoing stimulus for most children and not speed of processing or assimilation per se.

The reliability of the visual attentiveness score was assessed using data from the pilot study described earlier. The 2-week test-retest correlation was strong ($r[29] = .72$, $p < .01$).

MEMORY FOR LOCATIONS

Because the protocol for progressing through the cups and delays was the same for each child and the procedure was discontinued when the child failed on two successive trials, the total number of correct responses across trials could be used as an index of the ability to remember locations. This score ranged between 0 and 10. For example, an infant who found the hidden object in an array of two cups at a 10-second delay but failed twice on the next level (i.e., failed on four cups at a 1-second delay) would get a score of 3 (i.e., one point each for success on two cups at a 1-second delay, two cups at a 5-second delay, and two cups at a 10-second delay). The modal memory scores were 4, 7, and 8 at 14, 20, and 24 months, which reflected success through four cups at a 1-second delay, six cups at a 1-second delay, and six cups at a 5-second delay, respectively. The distribution of scores was relatively normal, except for a ceiling effect that emerged at 24 months.

Reliability for the memory score was assessed using data for 21 of the 31 pilot subjects described earlier. Memory performance was consistent across a 2-week interval ($r[19] = .62$, $p < .01$). The problem reported earlier for word-comprehension test reliability also affected the memory for locations test: some children resisted the experimenter's effort to resume a procedure that had become somewhat tedious 2 weeks earlier.

IX. RELATION AMONG DEPENDENT VARIABLES

In this chapter, we first use correlations among variables at each age to explore the relation among variables. We then use regression models to determine which variables offer the strongest prediction of MDI scores at each age and over time. Finally, we look at qualitative developmental function, defined as relative performance on nonverbal versus verbal variables and on expressive versus receptive variables.

CORRELATION AMONG VARIABLES AT EACH AGE

Table 2 contains the correlations among the dependent variables at each age. Because of the large number of degrees of freedom for each correlation, almost all values were statistically significant. Correlations on the basis of a data set that excluded any child with missing data on a particular variable were slightly lower, but the median difference at each age was only .01. Correlations were also virtually identical for the data set composed of subjects tested at home and in the laboratory at every age, with median differences of .03, .01, and .02 at 14, 20, and 24 months, respectively.

Inspection of the absolute values for the correlations in Table 2 indicated that the interrelations among the variables increased between 14 and 20 months. Eighteen of 21 correlations increased during this interval, many substantially. Sixteen of 21 correlations increased between 20 and 24 months, but the absolute change was generally minimal. Word comprehension, visual attentiveness, and memory for locations were relatively independent of the other measures at 14 months. However, word comprehension and visual attentiveness became increasingly related to the other measures at 20 and 24 months. Memory for locations remained relatively independent of the other measures across age. Separate correlations among the dependent variables at each age were calculated for males and females. Differences between correlations for males and females were negligible and within the range of chance variation that would be expected for 63 correlations.

TABLE 2

CORRELATIONS AMONG DEPENDENT VARIABLES AT EACH AGE

	NVB	EXP	REC	WC	ATTN	MEM
14 months:						
BSID MDI	.86**	.49**	.50**	.07	.10**	.15**
	(779)	(779)	(779)	(648)	(667)	(654)
Nonverbal		.33**	.38**	.11**	.05	.12**
		(786)	(786)	(654)	(673)	(661)
Verbal expressive			.43**	.13**	.12**	.13**
			(788)	(656)	(675)	(663)
Verbal receptive				.19**	.14**	.13**
				(656)	(673)	(663)
Word comprehension ...					−.04	.02
					(656)	(639)
Visual attentiveness						.13**
						(656)
20 months:						
BSID MDI	.78**	.70**	.69**	.30**	.25**	.15**
	(682)	(682)	(682)	(557)	(561)	(549)
Nonverbal		.36**	.48**	.18**	.18**	.11**
		(690)	(690)	(564)	(568)	(555)
Verbal expressive			.61**	.26**	.16**	.16**
			(703)	(567)	(572)	(558)
Verbal receptive				.37**	.26**	.16**
				(570)	(576)	(560)
Word comprehension ...					.09*	.09*
					(576)	(546)
Visual attentiveness						.14**
						(550)
24 months:						
BSID MDI	.76**	.73**	.71**	.32**	.30**	.22**
	(692)	(694)	(694)	(596)	(600)	(605)
Nonverbal		.40**	.48**	.17**	.24**	.18**
		(698)	(698)	(599)	(604)	(609)
Verbal expressive			.57**	.27**	.30**	.20**
			(703)	(604)	(609)	(614)
Verbal receptive				.26**	.28**	.18**
				(606)	(612)	(623)
Word comprehension ...					.11**	.14**
					(612)	(597)
Visual attentiveness						.07
						(602)

NOTE.—Values are Pearson product-moment correlations. Degrees of freedom are given in parentheses.
* $p < .05$.
** $p < .01$.

Expressive and receptive language had a strong positive relation at each age, comparable to results reported by others (e.g., Slomkowski et al., 1992, report a correlation of .51 between SICD expressive and receptive items at 2 years). However, because expressive and receptive scores were correlated with the MDI, the relation between them could be mediated by the child's general ability. To explore this possibility, we recalculated the correlations between expressive and receptive language at each age with the variance due to the nonverbal items on the MDI removed. These partial correlations were only slightly lower ($r[654] = .31$, $r[564] = .50$, and $r[599] = .57$ at 14, 20, and 24 months, respectively). This pattern suggests that, in its two guises, language ability rests on one or more shared processes that are not captured by nonverbal measures.

PREDICTING MDI SCORES

The MDI score was highly correlated with the verbal expressive, verbal receptive, and nonverbal constructs, but these correlations could reflect the overlap in items between the MDI and each of these measures. The correlations between the MDI and the measures not derived from the MDI were considerably lower. A stepwise regression model was used to determine which aspects of cognitive ability were most influential in predicting MDI scores. To derive assessments of expressive and receptive language that were not based on MDI questions, we recalculated these scores *using the SICD questions only*. These two variables (i.e., the average score on expressive and receptive items on the SICD as listed in Appendix A) were included along with scores on word comprehension, visual attentiveness, and memory for locations in a linear model used to predict MDI. As indicated in Table 3, expressive language and the cognitive variables accounted for some variance in MDI, but receptive language accounted for the largest proportion of variance in the MDI at each age and from early ages to later ages. This pattern of effects also held when regressions were calculated separately for males and females, for subjects with complete data on the relevant variables, and for subjects who participated in both home and laboratory visits at all three ages.

QUALITATIVE DEVELOPMENTAL FUNCTION

Qualitative developmental function refers to age-related stages of development. In a univariate context, this implies a sequence of related but qualitatively distinct abilities (e.g., the progression from babbling, to one-word speech, to multiword speech). In a multivariate context, qualitative developmental function can be viewed as a change in the behaviors that are considered the most prominent or salient aspect of the infant's ability. For example, in the McCall et al. (1977) study of transitions in early mental development, qualitative developmental function was defined on the basis of a description of the MDI items that were included in the first principal component.

A multivariate description of qualitative developmental function is arbi-

TABLE 3

CONTEMPORANEOUS AND DEVELOPMENTAL REGRESSION MODELS PREDICTING MDI

Step and Variable Entered	Partial R^2	F	df
Contemporaneous models:			
Predicting 14-month MDI from 14-month variables:			
1 Verbal receptive	.19	140.99	1, 621
2 Verbal expressive	.01	7.24	1, 620
3 Memory for locations	.01	6.56	
Predicting 20-month MDI from 20-month variables:			
1 Verbal receptive	.42	378.68	1, 525
2 Verbal expressive	.07	71.92	1, 524
Predicting 24-month MDI from 24-month variables:			
1 Verbal receptive	.42	418.27	1, 577
2 Verbal expressive	.07	79.68	1, 576
3 Word comprehension	.02	18.51	1, 575
4 Visual attentiveness	.01	11.80	1, 574
Developmental models:			
Predicting 20-month MDI from 14-month variables:			
1 Verbal receptive	.16	103.76	1, 560
2 Memory for locations	.03	22.86	1, 559
3 Verbal expressive	.02	11.29	1, 558
4 Visual attentiveness	.01	9.85	1, 557
Predicting 24-month MDI from 14-month variables:			
1 Verbal receptive	.14	90.99	1, 560
2 Visual attentiveness	.01	9.77	1, 559
Predicting 24-month MDI from 20-month variables:			
1 Verbal receptive	.32	219.72	1, 476
2 Verbal expressive	.04	27.62	1, 475
3 Word comprehension	.03	22.17	1, 474
4 Visual attentiveness	.02	12.18	1, 473

NOTE.—All F values in this table are significant at $p < .01$.

trary in that it will depend on the aspects of the child that are nominated and on how thoroughly and accurately each aspect is measured. However, given a particular set of aspects (e.g., the expressive, receptive, and nonverbal components), qualitative developmental function can be defined as the relation among these aspects, and relative comparisons can be made between the distributions of qualitative developmental functions for groups of subjects. More important, as will be described later, MZ and DZ twins can be compared to identify genetic and environmental influences.

Absolute differences among percentage correct scores for the nonverbal, expressive, and receptive constructs are arbitrary in that the specific values for each construct will depend on the difficulty of the set of items relevant at each age. However, when each construct at each age is converted to a z score, differences among z scores reflect the extent to which the child performed relatively well in a particular domain. We explored one aspect of qualitative developmental function by determining whether each child's highest

TABLE 4

NUMBER AND PERCENTAGE OF CHILDREN WHOSE HIGHEST SCORE IS NONVERBAL VERSUS
VERBAL (1) AND EXPRESSIVE VERSUS RECEPTIVE (2)

	(1)				(2)			
	Nonverbal		Verbal		Expressive		Receptive	
AGE AND SEX	N	%	N	%	N	%	N	%
14 Months	303	38	485	62	407	52	381	48
Male	176	44	223	56	207	52	192	48
Female	127	33	262	67	200	51	189	49
20 Months	240	35	452	65	375	54	317	46
Male	125	35	234	65	197	55	162	45
Female	115	34	218	66	178	54	155	47
24 Months	268	38	432	62	380	54	320	46
Male	141	40	215	60	193	54	163	46
Female	127	37	217	63	187	54	157	46

z score was on the nonverbal measure or on one of the verbal measures (i.e., either the expressive or the receptive score). We blurred the distinction between expressive and receptive language in this analysis to allow a broad determination of whether each child was relatively verbal or nonverbal. A child was designated *nonverbal* if the percentage correct z score was greater for the nonverbal construct than for both language constructs.

Table 4 lists the number and percentage of children in each classification at each age for the entire group and separately by sex. The highest score was most likely to be on the verbal measure for almost two-thirds of the children, and this proportion was significantly different from chance at each age ($\chi^2[1]$ = 21.30, 33.25, and 19.48, $p < .01$, respectively). The effect did not differ by age. One interpretation of this effect is that it reflects the baseline probability that one of the two language scores will be larger than the one nonverbal score. However, this interpretation is less plausible given the presence of a significant interaction: the distribution of highest score (i.e., nonverbal vs. verbal) differed significantly for males versus females at 14 months: more males than females had higher scores on the nonverbal measure, and more females than males had higher scores on a verbal measure ($\chi^2[1]$ = 10.94, $p < .01$).[11]

We also conducted a second analysis of qualitative developmental func-

---

[11] While z scores are sufficiently precise to ensure some detectable difference between adjacent scores, this difference can be relatively small. An additional analysis was conducted in which differences of less than .10 (which was roughly the tenth percentile in the distribution of differences between adjacent z scores) were set to missing. The pattern of coefficients for this and the subsequent analysis of MZ vs. DZ qualitative developmental function did not change.

tion in which we focused on the language variables per se and compared each child's z scores on the expressive and receptive measures. Each child was designated as *expressive* or *receptive* depending on which score was larger. The distribution of these scores is listed in Table 4. There was a slight tendency for children to score higher on the expressive questions, but the effect was not significant. There were no differences between the distributions for males and females at any age.

X. GROUP DIFFERENCES

In this section, we first explore group differences in age, sex, and zygosity, presenting group means and results from analyses of variance. We then examine quantitative change over time, with a focus on the patterns of change associated with each variable. Finally, we continue our exploration of quantitative change by using various parameters to capture aspects of individual growth functions.

EFFECTS OF AGE, SEX, AND ZYGOSITY

The means and standard deviations by sex for each variable at each age are listed in Table 5. Most of the variables in this study were created ad hoc, so there was no basis for comparing group means and standard deviations to existing data. However, for the MDI raw scores and the MDI, the values obtained here were comparable to those in previous work. Mean MDI scores were significantly above the expected score of 100, but this is not surprising given the demographic characteristics of our sample. The MDI is normed to have a mean of 100 and a standard deviation of 16. Given these values, the expected scores for the fifth and first percentile are 69 and 59. In the present sample, the fifth percentile scores were 82, 75, and 77 and the first percentile scores 65, 60, and 64 at 14, 20, and 24 months, respectively. These scores were at, or above, the expected values, suggesting few cases of retarded performance among the twins. Finally, the standard deviation on the MDI raw score for males and females combined was 5.51, 8.56, and 8.38 at 14, 20, and 24 months, respectively. These values were comparable to the standard deviations of 5.73, 6.05, and 8.62 reported for the Louisville Twin Study cohort at 12, 18, and 24 months, respectively (Wilson & Harpring, 1972). The similarity between these two sets of standard deviations suggests that administering the BSID in the home to both twins simultaneously did not cause excessive variability.

It is interesting to note that the variability in the BSID raw score in-

TABLE 5

SAMPLE SIZE, MEAN, AND STANDARD DEVIATION

VARIABLE AND AGE (Months)	MALE			FEMALE			ALL	
	N	M	SD	N	M	SD	M	SD
BSID raw:								
14	384	111.94	5.73	365	112.79	5.23	112.35	5.51
20	345	134.25	8.49	317	138.01	8.21	136.05	8.56
24	340	147.22	8.61	328	150.38	7.84	148.77	8.38
All		129.50	8.40		131.64	9.13		
BSID MDI:								
14	384	103.17	14.24	365	105.35	13.71	104.23	14.02
20	345	100.18	17.12	317	108.94	16.45	104.38	17.35
24	340	104.01	18.70	328	111.77	18.68	107.82	19.08
All		102.51	14.33		108.01	13.82		
Nonverbal:								
14	387	.63	.10	367	.63	.09	.63	.09
20	351	.67	.11	319	.70	.11	.68	.11
24	342	.76	.14	328	.80	.12	.78	.13
All		.68	.09		.70	.09		
Verbal expressive:								
14	388	.33	.12	368	.37	.13	.35	.12
20	354	.56	.23	327	.64	.23	.60	.23
24	343	.71	.21	330	.79	.18	.75	.20
All		.52	.16		.57	.17		
Verbal receptive:								
14	388	.28	.13	368	.32	.15	.30	.14
20	356	.55	.19	328	.63	.17	.59	.18
24	344	.69	.15	332	.74	.13	.71	.14
All		.49	.14		.54	.15		
Word comprehension:								
14	331	.35	.14	303	.35	.16	.35	.15
20	288	.44	.14	272	.49	.17	.46	.17
24	304	.47	.16	287	.48	.16	.47	.16
All		.41	.12		.43	.12		
Visual attentiveness:								
14	337	.53	.13	314	.53	.13	.53	.13
20	291	.59	.12	275	.58	.11	.58	.11
24	318	.57	.11	288	.59	.10	.58	.11
All		.56	.10		.56	.09		
Memory for locations:								
14	330	3.18	1.96	311	3.82	2.10	3.49	2.05
20	280	5.11	2.22	274	5.37	2.22	5.24	2.23
24	310	6.28	2.24	291	6.65	2.17	6.46	2.21
All		4.69	1.67		5.14	1.69		

creased significantly from earlier to later assessments for the Louisville Twin Study and for the present cohort ($F[298, 446] = 2.26$, $p < .01$, and $F[668, 749] = 2.31$, $p < .01$, respectively). This tendency is also obvious in the published norms for the MDI. From the perspective of the separate components of intelligence, the increase in variance from 14 to 24 months emerges because of increases in the variability of the nonverbal and expressive measures

TABLE 6

SIGNIFICANT AGE AND SEX EFFECTS

	F VALUE FOR EFFECT		
VARIABLE	Age	Sex	Age × Sex
BSID raw	5,357.63**	19.75**	8.33**
	(2, 616)	(1, 308)	(2, 616)
Pattern	14 < 20 < 24	M < F	M < F at 20 & 24
BSID MDI	14.22**	24.06**	8.50**
	(2, 616)	(1, 308)	(2, 616)
Pattern	14, 20 < 24	M < F	M < F at 20 & 24
BSID nonverbal	371.15**	7.37**	6.46**
	(2, 618)	(1, 309)	(2, 618)
Pattern	14 < 20 < 24	M < F	M < F at 20 & 24
Verbal expressive	934.01**	24.23**	4.69**
	(2, 622)	(1, 311)	(2, 622)
Pattern	14 < 20 < 24	M < F	M < F at 20 & 24
Verbal receptive	1,758.74**	26.91**	3.90*
	(2, 624)	(1, 312)	(2, 624)
Pattern	14 < 20 < 24	M < F	M < F at 20 & 24
Word comprehension	89.46**		3.34*
	(2, 454)		(2, 458)
Pattern	14 < 20, 24		M < F at 20
Visual attentiveness	36.27**		
	(2, 462)		
Pattern	14 < 20, 24		
Memory for locations	221.52**	6.57*	
	(2, 478)	(1, 239)	
Pattern	14 < 20 < 24	M < F	

NOTE.—Degrees of freedom are given in parentheses. Age effect patterns are based on planned contrasts of contiguous ages. Interaction effect patterns are based on planned contrasts of boys vs. girls at each age.
* $p < .05$.   ** $p < .01$.

($F[670, 754] = 2.11$, $p < .01$, and $F[673, 756] = 2.77$, $p < .01$, respectively). As noted above, norms from the MacArthur Communicative Development Inventories indicate an increasingly large range of individual differences for expressive language and a relatively narrower range for receptive language.

Effects of, and interactions among, age, sex, and zygosity were tested using a repeated-measures analysis of variance (ANOVA). Because measurements within a twin pair were not independent, the unit of analysis for each ANOVA was the family, with each twin randomly assigned as Twin 1 or Twin 2 and this variable then included as a within-subjects term in the model. As indicated in Table 6, there were significant effects of age for all variables, but age effects were notably smaller for the MDI (which is not surprising, given its age-based standardization) and the measures of word comprehension and visual attentiveness (which is not surprising, given that age-appropriate materials were used at each assessment). To examine effects of age for mental development as measured by the BSID, we also analyzed the MDI raw score, which reflected the number of mental items passed but was not expressed relative to age-specific norms.

The group means in Table 5 above were derived from all observations with data for that variable at that age, but the repeated-measures ANOVA reported in Table 6 excluded subjects missing data at any age. The values for means derived from this reduced set of observations were essentially identical to means derived from the entire sample, and the pattern of effects was exactly the same. Effects were also comparable for the set of subjects who completed both assessments at each age.

Age effects were generally linear, but some contiguous age differences were not statistically significant. Effects of sex emerged for most variables indicating better performance for females. For the MDI, the MDI raw score, expressive language, receptive language, the nonverbal construct, and the word-comprehension measure, sex interacted with age because of a tendency for sex differences to emerge or increase for older infants. The sex difference for the nonverbal construct was notably lower than effects for expressive or receptive language.

QUANTITATIVE DEVELOPMENTAL FUNCTIONS

Categories of Change

The main effects of age in Table 6 indicate that scores for cognitive measures increased across the second year, but inspection of individual scores revealed several discriminable patterns of development. We used statistical techniques (described later) to categorize each child's quantitative developmental function for the nonverbal, expressive, and receptive components. Note that this approach did not seem appropriate for the other variables. MDI scores were expressed in relation to norms. Normed IQ scores can reflect patterns of development over long time spans (McCall, Appelbaum, & Hogarty, 1973) or when the course of development is altered by intervention (Burchinal, Lee, & Ramey, 1989), but MDI scores are unlikely to reveal developmental function for a short-term cohort of normally developing children. The word-comprehension and visual attentiveness scores were derived from a different set of stimuli at each assessment age, so they were not appropriate for developmental function analysis. Memory for locations scores could be categorized into developmental functions, but the range of scores was too narrow to reveal reliable individual patterns.

Percentage correct scores for items designated as nonverbal, expressive,

TABLE 7

NUMBER AND PERCENTAGE OF CHILDREN IN EACH CATEGORY OF CHANGE

| | CHANGE | | | | | |
| | Early | | Continuous | | Late | |
VARIABLE AND SEX	N	%	N	%	N	%
Nonverbal	103	24	125	29	198	46
Male	46	22	57	27	105	50
Female	57	26	68	31	93	43
Verbal expressive	250	43	199	35	125	22
Male	117	41	101	35	70	24
Female	133	47	98	34	55	19
Verbal receptive	312	51	232	38	66	11
Male	151	48	121	38	44	14
Female	163	55	111	38	22	7

or receptive provide a measurement of each infant's ability level in a particular domain at various times and thus were amenable to developmental analysis on the basis of quantitative estimation of growth curves (Burchinal & Appelbaum, 1991). Obvious assumptions about the growth process and the limitation of only three assessment points urged a categorization of each infant into one of four patterns of growth. Specifically, we attempted to determine whether change was (*a*) greater between 14 and 20 months, (*b*) greater between 20 and 24 months, (*c*) the same for these two time intervals, or (*d*) absent (i.e., no change across trials). Because the interval between 14 and 20 months is longer than the interval between 20 and 24 months, we must be cautious in interpreting the absolute meaning of these patterns. However, the intervals were the same for all children, so a relative comparison of individual differences is feasible. The basis for categorization into quantitative developmental functions was the correlation between each child's three scores and a set of contrast weights that represented each pattern of change (i.e., for early change, the pattern was 1, 3, 3; for continuous change, the pattern was 1, 2, 3; and, for late change, the pattern was 1, 1, 3). For a description of this technique and some evidence supporting its efficacy, see Appendix B.

Given the pattern of effects in Table 6, we were particularly interested in the distribution of change for each measure (i.e., the basis for the age effects) and differences in the distribution of change for males and females. The percentage of infants with early, continuous, or late change in nonverbal, expressive, and receptive scores is listed in Table 7. Most infants with systematic change in their nonverbal scores had their greatest improvement in performance late (i.e., in the 20–24-month interval, $\chi^2[2] = 34.83$, $p < .01$), and the distribution was not different for males and females. This pattern is compatible with the means in Table 5 above, which suggest the greatest change in the nonverbal construct between 20 and 24 months. Infants whose expressive or receptive language scores changed were more likely to improve early (i.e., between 14 and 20 months, $\chi^2[2] = 41.30$, $p < .01$, and $\chi^2[2] = 154.90$, $p < .01$, respectively). This also fits the pattern in Table 5: language scores increased most between 14 and 20 months. There was no difference for males and females on the expressive score, but males showed less change early and more change late on the receptive score ($\chi^2[2] = 7.31$, $p < .05$). Finally, the distribution of type of change was different for the expressive compared with the receptive construct ($\chi^2[2] = 26.52$, $p < .01$), with more receptive change early and more expressive change late. This finding is compatible with the well-established fact that receptive language development precedes expressive language development.

Growth Functions

The categorization of each infant on the basis of whether change was concentrated between 14 and 20 months or between 20 and 24 months or was equal at both intervals has intuitive appeal because of its relation to the effects listed in Table 6 above and theoretical issues regarding early change versus late change. However, alternative measures of quantitative developmental function can be calculated that have other bases for appeal. For example, regression techniques can be used to determine the parameters of each child's growth function for each measure. Three points provide a relatively meager portrait of development, but the resulting parameters are continuous and thus amenable to a wider array of statistical tests than are the categories of change described earlier. Moreover, mathematical functions have proved to be particularly effective for describing early development in the lexicon (Bates & Carnevale, 1993; Huttenlocher et al., 1991).

Given the range of functions described earlier, we adopted a procrustean approach and calculated a linear coefficient across each child's scores at 14, 20, and 24 months regressed on the weights -1, 0, $+1$. Average coefficients calculated separately for the nonverbal, expressive, and receptive measures are .59, .81, and .89, respectively. A large coefficient indicates strong fit with the monotonic function. The mean linear coefficients differ across measure ($F[2, 1,264] = 124.68$, $p < .01$). Post hoc tests indicate that the mean linear coefficient was significantly lower for the nonverbal measure than for either language measure.

The psychological interpretation of the mean linear coefficient is obscure, but the measure seems to reflect both the shape and the range of change. Linear coefficients were lowest for the nonverbal measure because many children had no change and because the range of values was small. This

61

interpretation suggests the need for one additional measure of qualitative developmental function: each child's range of scores across age for each measure. The average range was lower for the nonverbal measure than for either language measure ($F[2, 1,628] = 736.34$, $p < .01$, with mean ranges of .17, .38, and .38 for nonverbal, expressive, and receptive, respectively). As will be described later, the main utility of the linear coefficient and the range emerge in comparisons of MZ and DZ twins.

XI. INDIVIDUAL DIFFERENCES

We first explore several specific influences that may affect individual differences: birth weight, assessment age, parents' education, and the physical similarity of DZ twins. We then use cross-age correlations to describe the stability of individual differences over time. We augment this analysis with an investigation of the extent to which individual children tend to have the same pattern of change over time.

INFLUENCES ON INDIVIDUAL DIFFERENCES

Birth Weight

Individual differences in birth weight are often related to differences in cognitive performance. This fact is particularly salient here because twins tend to have lower birth weights than singletons. The cohort in this study was selectively sampled to reduce this tendency but, as noted earlier, still contained a significant number of twins with relatively low birth weight. The correlation between birth weight and Bayley MDI scores was significant at each age, but its magnitude decreased ($r[765] = .23$, $r[672] = .18$, and $r[687] = .13$, respectively). This apparent decrease in correlation over time, in addition to the increase in MDI score noted earlier, is compatible with Wilson's (1977) contention on the basis of Louisville Twin Study data that there is a "catch-up" effect for low-birth-weight twins. However, it is also important to note that the magnitude of the relation between birth weight and MDI observed here is approximately two-thirds of the values reported for the Louisville Twin Study—an interpolation from figure 1 in Wilson (1985) suggests birth weight/MDI correlations of .32, .24, and .20 at 14, 20, and 24 months, respectively. This trend toward larger correlations in the Louisville data is probably due to the larger range of birth weights for twins in that study.

TABLE 8

<small>MID-PARENT EDUCATION CORRELATIONS WITH MID-TWIN COGNITIVE MEASURES</small>

Variable	14 Months	20 Months	24 Months	14 vs. 20
BSID MDI	.13**	.39**	.34**	3.76**
	(387)	(343)	(345)	
Nonverbal	.08	.24**	.25**	2.15*
	(388)	(343)	(346)	
Verbal expressive	.14**	.24**	.24**	1.35
	(388)	(347)	(347)	
Verbal receptive	.10	.29**	.27**	2.70**
	(388)	(347)	(348)	
Word comprehension	.12*	.38**	.27**	3.46**
	(331)	(288)	(306)	
Visual attentiveness	.15**	.18**	.20**	.37
	(334)	(289)	(306)	
Memory for locations	.14**	.06	.11*	.99
	(335)	(291)	(315)	

<small>NOTE.—Values are Pearson product-moment correlations. Degrees of freedom are given in parentheses. Comparison of 14 vs. 20 correlations is based on one-tailed z scores.</small>
<small>* $p < .05$.</small>
<small>** $p < .01$.</small>

Assessment Age

Given the strong effects of age on each variable, it is also relevant to determine whether the range of age *within each age bracket* was related to performance. The MDI is age adjusted and is therefore not relevant for this analysis, but the MDI raw score was significantly related to age at the home visit for each age bracket ($r[778] = .19$, $r[681] = .09$, and $r[691] = .11$ at 14, 20, and 24 months, respectively). The weak relation was significant for expressive, receptive, and nonverbal constructs at 14 months but only for the nonverbal construct at 20 and 24 months. There was no relation between age at the laboratory visit and performance on any procedure. Thus, as would be expected given the main effect of age, age of testing accounts for a statistically significant portion of variance at each age group. However, the absolute values of the correlations are small, accounting for only 1%–4% of the total variance.

Parents' Education

Individual differences in parents' education are likely to be related to the child's cognitive performance. We explored this relation through correlations between the mid-twin score on each variable and the mid-parent score for years of education. The correlation matrix, presented in Table 8, suggested low positive correlations at 14 months and somewhat stronger correlations at 20 and 24 months for most measures. The statistical significance of this developmental trend was assessed by comparing correlations for contiguous ages using one-tailed tests based on Fisher's transformation to z. This analysis indicated that mid-parent to mid-twin correlations increased between 14 and 20 months for the MDI, nonverbal, receptive, and word-comprehension scores. (For values, see Table 8.) Mid-parent to mid-twin correlations for males and females were comparable. We also computed a correlation matrix for children with complete data on each measure and across all measures. The values for correlations tended to be smaller, particularly for language measures, but the median value of the difference was only .02 for subjects with complete data on the relevant measure and .04 for subjects with data from all assessments. The only change in the pattern of significant effects was that the word-comprehension correlation at 14 months failed to attain statistical significance in both new calculations.

Physical Similarity

MZ twins are more physically similar than DZ twins. This fact could color the interpretation of twin correlations *if* physical similarity evokes more similar treatment (i.e., evokes a more similar environment). We do not have a direct measurement of the environment for twins in this study, but we do have a way to test the hypothesis that physical similarity influences behavior. As noted earlier, physical similarity was assessed for each pair of twins as a means of determining zygosity: twins who are similar across a range of physical attributes are likely to be MZ. The distribution of similarity scores across MZ and DZ twins (see Figure 1) reveals the presence of two distinct groups: the MZ twins contribute to a marked peak at the score that reflects maximal similarity, and the DZ twins lie in a relatively normal distribution of similarity with a mean score suggesting a relatively low degree of similarity. Zygosity assessment is straightforward for scores central to each of these two distributions but is problematic at the point where the more similar tail of the DZ distribution overlaps with the less similar edge of the MZ distribution.

What can be learned from the distribution of physical similarity for DZ twins? Like any two siblings, DZ twins share 50% of their segregating genes, but random segregation of chromosomes into gametes produces a range of genetic and phenotypic similarity. If the behavioral similarity of DZ twins can be predicted by their physical similarity, this could be interpreted in either genetic or environmental terms. From a genetic perspective, physical similarity in DZ twins could be a proxy for underlying genetic similarity that affects behavior. From the environmental perspective, if parents treat twins similarly because they look the same, DZ twins with strong physical similarity could have more similar environments than DZ twins who do not look the same.

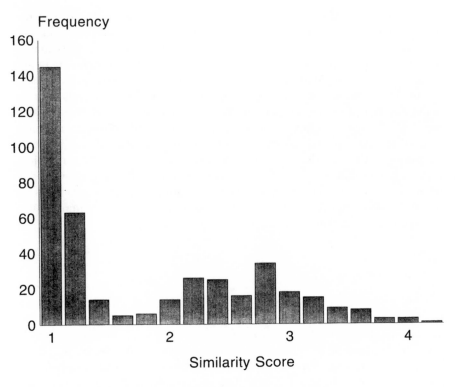

FIGURE 1.—Average physical similarity of MZ and DZ twin pairs

To explore the relation between physical and behavioral similarity in DZ twins, we created an average physical similarity score for each DZ twin pair by averaging across all similarity ratings available at 14, 20, and 24 months. A behavioral similarity rating was created by converting the outcome variables to standard scores, calculating the absolute value of the difference between DZ twins on each variable, and averaging these absolute differences across ages. For conceptual clarity, two behavioral similarity ratings were created— a general rating derived from the MDI and a specific rating derived from each variable.

Two approaches to analysis were used. In the first, the correlation between DZ physical similarity and either index of behavioral similarity approached zero for all analyses. In the second, a comparison between the 25% most physically similar DZ twins and the 25% least physically similar DZ twins indicated no difference on either index of behavioral similarity. More detailed analyses of individual constructs and age-specific ratings of physical similarity were conducted, but the interpretation of the statistical significance of individual results is problematic within the context of this large set of correla-

TABLE 9

CROSS-TIME CORRELATIONS

Variable	14–24 Months	14–20 Months	20–24 Months	Compare 14–20 and 20–24 Months
BSID MDI	.43**	.48**	.67**	5.27**
	(666)	(661)	(635)	
Nonverbal	.32**	.38**	.49**	2.54*
	(674)	(673)	(645)	
Verbal expressive	.31**	.37**	.58**	4.90**
	(681)	(687)	(656)	
Verbal receptive	.40**	.45**	.63**	4.54**
	(684)	(690)	(662)	
Word comprehension	.08	.13**	.24**	1.77
	(527)	(513)	(512)	
Visual attentiveness	.28**	.30**	.37**	1.29
	(544)	(531)	(521)	
Memory for locations	.05	.04	.17**	2.10*
	(544)	(510)	(513)	

NOTE.—Values are Pearson product-moment correlations. Degrees of freedom are given in parentheses. Comparison of 14–20 and 20–24 correlations is based on one-tailed z scores.
* $p < .05$.
** $p < .01$.

tions and t tests. To limit the possibility of Type 1 errors, we adopted a relatively conservative probability level of $p < .01$. The results were consistent with the pattern of no relation between DZ physical similarity and DZ behavioral similarity—except for one intriguing anomaly. At 14 months, DZ twins who were more physically similar had greater performance similarity on the memory for locations test ($r[138] = .25$, $p < .01$). Also, the DZ twins who were among the 25% most physically similar twin pairs had smaller absolute differences in memory for locations score than did DZ twins among the 25% least physically similar twin pairs ($t[66] = 3.14$, $p < .01$).

STABILITY OF INDIVIDUAL DIFFERENCES

Table 9 lists cross-time correlations measuring continuity in individual differences across the second year. The absolute values of these phenotypic correlations suggested some stability for all measures except word comprehension and memory for locations, but within a broader context of considerable change. Longitudinal phenotypic stability averaged .37, which leaves 86% of the cross-time variance unaccounted for. Continuity between 20 and 24 months was notably larger than continuity between 14 and 20 months for every variable. One-tailed tests of this difference based on z scores (reported in Table 9) were statistically significant for five of seven comparisons. Separate correlations for MZ and DZ twin types and for males and females revealed a comparable pattern for each subgroup. Correlations for the subset of subjects with no missing data were comparable: the median difference was 0 for subjects missing data on a measure and .01 for the cohort with both assessments at all three ages. Despite the increased magnitude of the present sample, cross-time correlations were essentially identical to values reported previously by Plomin et al. (1993).

An alternative approach to stability of individual differences is to determine whether individual children tended to have the same quantitative developmental function (i.e., pattern of change) across measures. Each comparison between developmental functions produces a cross-classification grid in which the developmental functions for one measure are the rows and the developmental functions for the other measure are the columns. Stability is indicated if cross-classifications tend to lie on the diagonal. This relation can be indexed with a contingency coefficient, C (Siegel, 1956). Quantitative developmental functions were classified as early change, continuous change, or late change, as described earlier and in Appendix B, for the nonverbal, expressive, and receptive constructs. Children classified as no change or indeterminate change were eliminated from this analysis.

The cross-classification of quantitative developmental function was related for expressive and receptive constructs ($C = .33$, $p < .01$), for receptive and nonverbal constructs ($C = .26$, $p < .01$), but not for expressive and nonverbal constructs ($C = .15$). These values replicate the pattern of correlations among constructs reported in Table 2 above: expressive language and receptive language were more strongly correlated with each other than either was correlated with the nonverbal measure, and receptive language was more strongly correlated with the nonverbal measure than was the expressive language measure. Despite the finding noted earlier that the general distribution of developmental function is different for expressive and receptive constructs, individuals tend to show the same pattern and to do so more for expressive and receptive language than for either aspect of language compared with the nonverbal construct, particularly for expressive language compared with the nonverbal construct.

XII. GENETIC AND ENVIRONMENTAL INFLUENCES

Heritability (h^2) reflects the extent to which variance in behavior can be attributed to genetic influence. Shared, or common, environmental variation (labeled c^2) is the twin resemblance that is not explained by hereditary resemblance. Finally, unique or nonshared environmental variance (labeled e^2) is composed of influences that contribute to the uniqueness of each twin. Genetic and environmental influences are revealed by comparisons of MZ and DZ twins under the general assumption that genetic influences make MZ twins more similar than DZ twins, that shared environment makes MZ and DZ twins equally similar, and that unique environment makes MZ twins different from one another.

As a preliminary approach for identifying genetic and environmental influences, we present MZ and DZ intraclass correlations for the entire sample and separately for males and females. We then use a model to estimate genetic and environmental parameters. Our analysis of continuity and change is launched with a presentation of cross-age correlations, followed by a Cholesky decomposition on each variable across age to estimate genetic and environmental parameters. Change and continuity are also explored on the basis of comparisons by twin type of the indices of quantitative and qualitative developmental function. Finally, we explore continuity and change across measure at each age using cross-measure correlations and a series of Cholesky decompositions.

AGE-SPECIFIC INDIVIDUAL DIFFERENCES

Intraclass Correlations

Table 10 lists the MZ and DZ intraclass correlations for each measure at each age. Correlations for MZ and DZ twins were relatively high for the MDI and its components, but the magnitude of these correlations and the relation between MZ and DZ correlations varied across measure and across time. All

69

TABLE 10
Twin Intraclass Correlations

Variable	14 Months			20 Months			24 Months		
	MZ	DZ	MZ vs. DZ	MZ	DZ	MZ vs. DZ	MZ	DZ	MZ vs. DZ
BSID MDI	.58** (199)	.38** (169)	2.46*	.80** (174)	.64** (146)	3.18**	.83** (176)	.61** (152)	4.56**
Nonverbal	.54** (202)	.28** (172)	2.96**	.63** (179)	.35** (150)	3.58**	.67** (178)	.42** (153)	3.50**
Verbal expressive	.38** (203)	.37** (171)	.10	.76** (181)	.63** (156)	2.36*	.79** (179)	.60** (155)	3.61**
Verbal receptive	.64** (204)	.49** (172)	2.30*	.68** (183)	.61** (153)	1.18	.71** (178)	.62** (157)	1.54
Word comprehension	.06 (165)	.07 (141)	−.09	.23** (144)	.24** (128)	−.08	.26** (149)	.21** (138)	.50
Visual attentiveness	.54** (175)	.34** (142)	2.19*	.67** (147)	.33** (131)	4.12**	.62** (153)	.35** (140)	3.22**
Memory for locations	.27** (172)	.14* (139)	1.22	.27** (137)	.13* (127)	1.20	.16** (151)	.11 (138)	.42

Note.—Statistical tests for correlations are one tailed. Degrees of freedom are given in parentheses. Comparison of MZ and DZ correlations is based on one-tailed z scores.

* $p < .05$.

** $p < .01$.

but two (of 21) DZ correlations were significantly above chance, suggesting the presence of genetic and/or shared environmental effects. MZ correlations were significantly greater than DZ correlations at each age for the MDI, suggesting the presence of genetic effects, but this general statement was not true across all constructs. The nonverbal MDI questions and the visual attentiveness scores suggested genetic effects at each assessment. MZ-DZ differences for memory for locations were in the direction of genetic effects, but the differences were not significant. Expressive language correlations suggested a genetic influence late in the second year. The receptive language measure indicated heritability at 14 months; the word-comprehension score indicated no genetic effect.

Correlations on the subset of infants with no missing data on a specific variable were only slightly different, with a median discrepancy of .02 at each age from the correlations listed in Table 10. There was no obvious direction of difference for MZ versus DZ twins or across age. Correlations on the subset tested at every age were also comparable, with median differences of .03, .02, and .05 at 14, 20, and 24 months, respectively, as compared to the full sample. There was one notable trend: subjects in the full data set had lower DZ correlations at 24 months, with a median difference of .09 when compared to the values in Table 10.

MZ and DZ intraclass correlations were calculated separately by sex, and these correlations are presented in Table 11.[12] The correlations for males and females were similar in many cases, but the direction of difference was consistent for each type of twin: for MZ twins, 62% of male correlations were larger than female correlations; for DZ twins, 71% of female correlations were larger than male correlations. Patterns of statistical significance were often convergent for males and females, but there were a few points of marked divergence, particularly for the laboratory measures. The general picture that emerges is of various age-specific and possibly sex-specific genetic and environmental effects for each measure. The MZ-DZ differences on the MDI were significant for males at all three assessments, but they were significant for females at 24 months only. A casual comparison of differences in genetic effects for males and females suggests that this pattern can be explained as the lack of a genetic effect on the nonverbal items for females at 14 months and the lack of a genetic effect on the expressive items for females at 20 and 24 months. Females also had no genetic effect for the measure of receptive language at 24 months. Male-female differences on the laboratory measures were less

---

[12] Inspection of the scatter plots for twin scores for each zygosity group × sex combination revealed the presence of some outlying scores that were not apparent when zygosity group and sex were combined. We eliminated five data points (four at 14 months and one at 20 months) that met the criterion of being greater than 2 standard deviations beyond their nearest neighbor.

TABLE 11

TWIN INTRACLASS CORRELATIONS SEPARATED FOR MALES AND FEMALES

VARIABLE AND SEX	14 MONTHS			20 MONTHS			24 MONTHS		
	MZ	DZ	MZ vs. DZ	MZ	DZ	MZ vs. DZ	MZ	DZ	MZ vs. DZ
BSID MDI:									
Male	.59** (94)	.27** (83)	2.61*	.83** (83)	.54** (80)	4.01**	.86** (82)	.59** (82)	4.21**
Female	.57** (103)	.50** (74)	.64	.74** (88)	.67** (64)	.83	.79** (91)	.60** (68)	2.45*
Nonverbal:									
Male	.61** (96)	.29** (93)	2.91**	.67** (87)	.29** (83)	3.46**	.64** (84)	.40** (82)	2.28*
Female	.42** (103)	.32** (76)	.78	.66** (88)	.38** (65)	2.51*	.69** (91)	.43** (68)	2.57*
Verbal expressive:									
Male	.29** (97)	.38** (93)	−.68	.76** (87)	.57** (85)	2.45*	.80** (84)	.53** (82)	3.48**
Female	.54** (104)	.33** (76)	1.69	.72** (90)	.68** (69)	.49	.76** (92)	.68** (69)	1.05

Verbal receptive:									
Male	.63** (97)	.45** (93)	1.90	.70** (89)	.54*** (85)	1.94	.75** (84)	.58** (84)	2.23*
Female	.62** (104)	.51** (76)	1.24	.60** (90)	.66** (70)	−.68	.63** (92)	.64** (70)	−.06
Word comprehension:									
Male	.00 (85)	.08 (75)	−.50	.23** (70)	.21* (68)	.11	.12 (71)	.13 (74)	−.06
Female	.11 (78)	.22* (64)	−.64	.20* (72)	.25** (58)	−.33	.38** (76)	.34** (62)	.29
Visual attentiveness:									
Male	.52** (87)	.48** (77)	.38	.64** (71)	.35** (70)	2.38*	.62** (73)	.47** (76)	1.43
Female	.55** (85)	.14 (67)	2.88**	.70** (73)	.30** (59)	3.29**	.62** (77)	.08 (62)	3.84**
Memory for locations:									
Male	.28** (87)	−.05 (71)	2.08*	.28** (64)	.20* (66)	.50	.13 (73)	.15 (74)	−.12
Female	.20** (82)	.33** (65)	−.83	.26** (70)	.05 (59)	1.22*	.17* (75)	.04 (63)	.74

NOTE.—Statistical tests for correlations are one tailed. Degrees of freedom are given in parentheses. Comparison of MZ and DZ correlations is based on one-tailed z scores.

* $p < .05$.

** $p < .01$.

systematic, but females tended to show stronger genetic effects than males on the measure of visual attentiveness.

Estimating h^2, c^2, and e^2

Univariate estimates of h^2, c^2, and e^2 were computed according to the model described by DeFries and Fulker (1988) and extended by Cyphers, Phillips, Fulker, and Mrazek (1990). The following model was fit to the data from MZ and DZ twin pairs simultaneously:

$$P_1 = B_1S + B_2P_2 + B_3R + B_4P_2R + A,$$

where P_1 is Twin 1's score, S is the sex of the twin pair ($S = 0$ for females, and $S = 1$ for males), P_2 is Twin 2's score, R is the coefficient of relationship of the twins ($R = 1.0$ for MZ twins, and $R = 0.5$ for DZ twins), P_2R is the product of the coefficient of relationship and Twin 2's score, and A is the regression constant. In this model, B_1 is the partial regression of one twin's score on sex and removes variance due to sex from the other parameter estimates. B_2, the partial regression of one twin's score on the co-twin's score, estimates c^2; B_3 is a correction term for mean differences between MZ and DZ twins; and B_4 estimates h^2.

Twin data were entered twice to permit the scores of each twin to serve in turn as outcome value and as predictor. To correct for the doubled sample size, standard errors for the regression coefficients were adjusted by

$$\sqrt{(2N - k - 1)/(N - k - 1)},$$

where N is the number of twin families, and k is the number of regression predictors.

A statistically significant parameter implies that parameter's nonzero contribution to individual variation for the phenotype, but the statistical significance of each parameter depends on how it is calculated. The significant genetic parameter depends on the difference between two correlations and thus is relatively insensitive. For the sample size tested here, the genetic parameter must be greater than approximately 0.30 to be statistically significant. This constitutes a relatively stringent test and suggests that genetic effects must be quite robust to be detected here. The shared environment parameter reflects twin similarity regardless of zygosity and thus is relatively robust. The critical value for the shared environment parameter here is approximately 0.12. We did not assess the statistical significance of the parameter for unique environment because it is estimated in the DeFries and Fulker model as a residual term after variance is removed that can be attributed to genetic and shared environmental effects.

TABLE 12

ESTIMATES OF GENETIC (h^2) AND SHARED ENVIRONMENTAL (c^2) VARIANCE AT EACH AGE

VARIABLE	14 MONTHS		20 MONTHS		24 MONTHS	
	h^2	c^2	h^2	c^2	h^2	c^2
BSID MDI..................	.39*	.19	.34*	.45*	.45*	.37*
	(.18)	(.14)	(.15)	(.12)	(.15)	(.12)
Nonverbal...................	.52*	.02	.55*	.07	.50*	.16
	(.19)	(.15)	(.19)	(.15)	(.18)	(.15)
Verbal expressive.............	.01	.35*	.25	.49*	.38*	.40*
	(.19)	(.15)	(.16)	(.13)	(.15)	(.13)
Verbal receptive..............	.28*	.34*	.13	.52*	.18	.51*
	(.17)	(.14)	(.16)	(.13)	(.16)	(.13)
Word comprehension.........	.00	.07	.00	.22*	.08	.17
		(.06)		(.06)	(.23)	(.18)
Visual attentiveness...........	.39*	.14	.67*	.00	.54*	.07
	(.20)	(.16)	(.06)		(.20)	(.16)
Memory for locations.........	.24*	.00	.27*	.00	.10	.05
	(.07)		(.07)		(.23)	(.18)

NOTE.—Statistical tests for h^2 and c^2 are one tailed. A parameter of .00 indicates use of constrained model. Standard errors corrected for double entry are given in parentheses.

* $p < .05$.

Twin contrast effects, nonadditive genetic influence, and random fluctuations in the sampling distribution of MZ and DZ twin correlations can result in a c^2 that is negative (i.e., the DZ twin correlation is larger than the MZ twin correlation) or an h^2 that exceeds 1.0 (i.e., the MZ twin correlation is more than double the DZ twin correlation). Estimates of h^2 and c^2 were constrained to lie between their theoretical lower and upper bounds of 0.0 and 1.0 by excluding h^2 or c^2 terms that were negative and fitting a reduced regression model under the constraint that the omitted term does not account for any phenotypic variance. Cherny, DeFries, and Fulker (1992) have demonstrated that these constrained tests of h^2 and c^2 are unbiased and provide estimates similar to those obtained on the basis of conventional model-fitting procedures. If h^2 is excluded, then the estimate for c^2 is a weighted average of the twin resemblance for MZ and DZ pairs (after correction for sex and zygosity effects). If c^2 is dropped, then h^2 is still estimated with a model in which DZ twins are expected to have half the degree of resemblance of MZ twins, but the MZ twin resemblance becomes an upper bound for h^2 (i.e., these twins are made similar only by genetic influences). Furthermore, because DZ twins are less than half as similar as MZ twins (i.e., c^2 was negative), the pooled average will be less than the MZ resemblance (unless the DZ twins contribute no information relative to the MZ twins).

The parameters for h^2 and c^2 for each variable at each age are presented in Table 12. Figure 2 presents pie charts in which variance is partitioned into

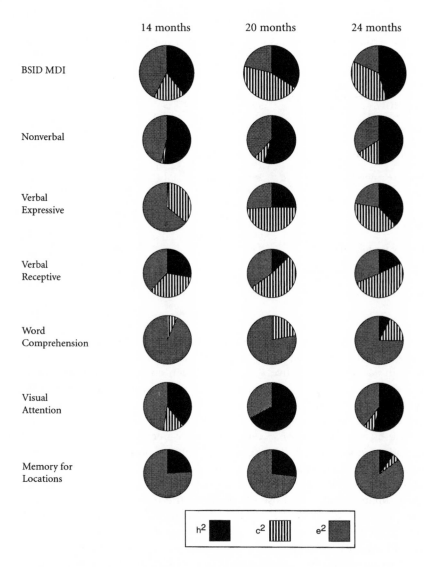

14 months   20 months   24 months

BSID MDI

Nonverbal

Verbal
Expressive

Verbal
Receptive

Word
Comprehension

Visual
Attention

Memory for
Locations

h^2 ■ c^2 ▥ e^2 ▨

FIGURE 2.—Age-specific estimates of h^2, c^2, and e^2 for each outcome variable

these three components for each measure at each assessment age. One-tailed
t tests were used to evaluate the statistical significance of each calculated parameter relative to its standard error.

The heritability estimates here generally replicate and extend previously
reported estimates calculated on the first 200 pairs of twins for the present
cohort tested at 14 and 20 months (Plomin et al., 1993). For the MDI at 14

months, MZ and particularly DZ twin correlations drifted lower, causing a reduction in the size of c^2. With this larger sample, h^2 remained significant. The twin correlations at 20 months were virtually unchanged and suggested significant effects of genes and environment. The present data indicate that the significant effects of genetics and environment on MDI continue through 24 months.

For the language measures, items based on parent report have been eliminated from the SICD, which tended to reduce the magnitude of the twin correlations, but the general pattern of shared environmental effects on language remained similar to our previous report: significant shared environmental effects on expressive and receptive language at each assessment. However, genetic effects were notably different: we found significant h^2 for the receptive construct at 14 months and the expressive construct at 24 months. Plomin et al. (1993) found significant genetic effects on receptive language at 20 months, but that effect was weak here and absent at 24 months. The general conclusion for the receptive construct and the word-comprehension score is the same: any genetic effect on receptive language is transitory at best. Word-comprehension correlations were very low compared with the previous report owing to a change in our approach to scoring the data. The word-comprehension score used in this study reflects the percentage correct rather than the total number of words correct. This latter measure is affected by the infant's attentiveness, and, as would be expected, the results for visual attentiveness are comparable to the previously reported results for word comprehension.

The effects of heritability on nonverbal MDI items and visual attentiveness were the most consistent across age, with impressive h^2 values at each age and low values for c^2. Memory for locations correlations at 14 months replicated our previous report suggesting a genetic effect, but the MZ correlation at 20 months increased, causing a significant value of h^2 at that age as well. The twin correlations for memory for locations at 24 months were relatively low.

Sex Differences in Estimates of Genetic and Environmental Effects

Table 11 above suggests discrepancies between the MZ and the DZ twin correlations for males and females at some ages, so we calculated the genetic and environmental effects separately for males and females. This was accomplished through separate runs of the DeFries and Fulker model for males and females on each measure. The parameters for these sex-specific genetic and environmental effects are presented in Table 13. An interesting pattern emerged for infants at the two youngest assessment ages: the analysis of MDI indicated heritable effects for males and environmental effects for females.

TABLE 13

Estimates of Genetic (h^2) and Shared Environment (c^2) Variance at Each Age Separated for Males and Females

VARIABLE AND SEX	14 Months		20 Months		24 Months	
	h^2	c^2	h^2	c^2	h^2	c^2
BSID MDI:						
Male.....................	.58*	.00	.58*	.25	.55*	.31*
	(.08)		(.22)	(.18)	(.21)	(.17)
Female..................	.14	.43*	.14	.60*	.38	.41*
	(.25)	(.20)	(.23)	(.18)	(.23)	(.18)
Nonverbal:						
Male.....................	.60*	.00	.65*	.00	.48*	.15
	(.07)		(.08)		(.25)	(.21)
Female..................	.32	.11	.37	.20	.53*	.16
	(.28)	(.21)	(.28)	(.23)	(.25)	(.21)
Verbal expressive:						
Male.....................	.00	.28*	.39*	.37*	.52*	.27
		(.07)	(.23)	(.18)	(.23)	(.18)
Female..................	.40	.13	.09	.64*	.18	.59*
	(.27)	(.21)	(.23)	(.18)	(.23)	(.20)
Verbal receptive:						
Male.....................	.37	.27	.32	.38*	.33	.42*
	(.24)	(.20)	(.24)	(.20)	(.23)	(.18)
Female..................	.21	.41*	.00	.63*	.00	.63*
	(.24)	(.20)		(.06)		(.06)
Word comprehension:						
Male.....................	.00	.00	.03	.20	.00	.15
			(.32)	(.25)		(.11)
Female..................	.00	.16*	.00	.22*	.08	.30
		(.08)		(.08)	(.31)	(.25)
Visual attentiveness:						
Male.....................	.07	.45*	.58*	.07	.30	.32
	(.27)	(.21)	(.28)	(.24)	(.27)	(.21)
Female..................	.51*	.00	.69*	.00	.57*	.00
	(.08)		(.08)		(.08)	
Memory for locations:						
Male.....................	.21*	.00	.16	.12	.00	.14*
	(.10)		(.34)	(.27)		(.08)
Female..................	.00	.25*	.24*	.00	.15	.00
		(.08)	(.10)		(.10)	

Note.—Statistical tests for h^2 and c^2 are one tailed. Parameter of .00 indicates use of constrained model. Standard errors corrected for double entry are given in parentheses.

* $p < .05$.

This pattern reflected differences in the components at these two ages. Males had larger h^2 values than females for the nonverbal measure and most comparisons of expressive and receptive language. Females had larger c^2 values than males for the nonverbal measure and most comparisons of expressive and receptive language. The pattern for visual attentiveness was the opposite—males had larger c^2 values, and females had larger h^2 values. Genetic and environmental parameters calculated for word comprehension and memory for locations were too small to be useful. By 24 months, the correlations for males and females were more similar to each other, except for expressive language: males had a notably larger h^2, and females had a notably larger c^2.

Note that the reduction in sample size boosted the standard error so that the statistical significance of differences between males and females on each parameter became questionable. To assess the significance of sex as a source of variance, we recalculated the full-cohort DeFries and Fulker model for each variable to include parameters for interaction effects. Specifically, three parameters were added: B_5 is the interaction of sex and zygosity; B_6 is the interaction of sex and the score for Twin 2, which reflects the interaction between sex and c^2; and B_7 is the three-way interaction of sex, zygosity, and the score for Twin 2, which reflects the interaction between sex and h^2. B_6 was statistically significant for the MDI score at 14 months, and B_7 was statistically significant for the expressive language score at 14 months, but these effects were small and isolated. Both parameters were statistically significant for the attentiveness score at 14 and 24 months, suggesting a robust interaction for that variable only. Thus, although these data hint at sex-specific effects of h^2 and c^2, the sample size may be too small to provide a robust statistical test of this intriguing possibility.

LONGITUDINAL CONTINUITY AND CHANGE

Age-specific analyses partition variance into components that are associated with heredity, shared environment, and unique environment at each assessment age. From a developmental perspective, it is useful to go beyond this age-specific analysis and ask broader multivariate questions regarding the extent to which each type of variance should be attributed to a single factor over time (continuity) or to a set of factors emerging at different times (change). There is some overlap between the univariate and the multivariate perspectives: If there is little variance attributed to a particular partition (e.g., the low values of c^2 at each age for the MDI-based nonverbal measure), then there is no variance to be explained by continuity or change. However, if there is even a moderate amount of variance, then continuity, change, or both are plausible, and a technique is needed to find the best explanation.

Cross-Age Correlations

As a first step toward exploring the continuity and change of the influences on variance in the phenotypic similarity of twins, we estimated cross-age correlations for genetic variance (R_g), shared environmental variance

(R_c), and unique environmental variance (R_e) on each dependent variable. These correlations estimate the extent to which the variance that can be attributed to a specific influence is shared between pairs of assessment ages. Shared variance implies continuity; the lack of covariation implies change. Consider the genetic correlation, which is the correlation between the genetic effects on a trait at Time 1 and the genetic effects on that trait at Time 2. If the genetic effects at Time 1 correlate perfectly with the genetic effects at Time 2, then the genetic correlation will be 1.0, and continuity is obvious. If the genetic effects at Time 1 are independent of the genetic effects at Time 2, then the genetic correlation will be 0, and there is evidence for genetic change.

The computational leverage to assess genetic and environmental cross-age correlations comes from the cross-twin correlation, which is the correlation between Twin 1's score at Time 1 and Twin 2's score at Time 2. Doubling the difference between MZ and DZ twin cross-correlations estimates the genetic contribution to stability, and comparable approaches can be used to estimate environmental influences on stability. However, to make maximal use of subjects with missing data, we estimated cross-age correlations for genetic variance, shared environmental variance, and unique environmental variance using the Cholesky decomposition of variance, which will be described in detail later. The Cholesky decomposition provides estimates comparable to the cross-twin correlation but imposes certain regularities on these correlations (e.g., discounting instances where DZ cross-twin correlations are higher than MZ, under the criterion that all sources of variance must be positive).

The interpretation of cross-age correlations must be tempered by knowledge of the importance of each source of variance for each individual dependent variable. For example, if there is relatively little genetic variance in a particular dependent variable, then strong shared genetic variance for that variable (i.e., a large genetic correlation) contributes little to phenotypic similarity. Table 14 lists the R_g, R_c, and R_e values for each variable, but we will focus only on the variables with notable age-specific effects at both ages (as indicated in Table 12 above).

There was a significant h^2 at each age for MDI, the nonverbal construct, and visual attentiveness. The genetic correlations for each of these variables (presented in Table 14) were strong for comparisons of 14 to 20 months, 14 to 24 months, and 20 to 24 months. This suggests the possibility of cross-age continuity in the genetic variance for MDI, the nonverbal construct, and visual attentiveness. Expressive language had notable genetic variance at 20 and 24 months and a strong genetic correlation for this age span, which suggests the possibility of cross-age continuity. Cross-age genetic correlations were high for some other variables, but heritabilities were low, precluding easy interpretation. For example, the large genetic correlations for word compre-

TABLE 14

Implied Matrix of Genetic (R_g), Shared Environment (R_c), and Unique Environment (R_e) Correlations across Age for Each Variable

VARIABLE AND AGE	GENETIC (R_g)		SHARED ENVIRONMENT (R_c)		UNIQUE ENVIRONMENT (R_e)	
	20 Months	24 Months	20 Months	24 Months	20 Months	24 Months
BSID MDI:						
14 months............	.57	.50	.78	.77	.12	.08
20 months...........		.66		1.00		−.07
Nonverbal:						
14 months...........	.50	.35	1.00	1.00	.06	.11
20 months...........		.74		1.00		−.02
Verbal expressive:						
14 months...........	.26	.59	.75	.66	.13	−.10
20 months...........		.81		.80		−.06
Verbal receptive:						
14 months...........	.63	.33	.71	.68	.01	.08
20 months...........		.94		.89		.03
Word comprehension:						
14 months...........	−1.00	−1.00	.97	.77	.01	−.01
20 months...........		1.00		.90		.04
Visual attentiveness:						
14 months...........	.71	.41	−.66	.52	.19	.05
20 months...........		.93		−.98		.08
Memory for locations:						
14 months...........	−.28	.13	1.00	.99	.07	−.02
20 months...........		.91		.98		−.03

hension (i.e., +1.00 and −1.00) are not informative because h^2 values for this variable are 0, 0, and .08 at 14, 20, and 24 months, respectively.

The c^2 values were significant at each age for both measures of language. Shared environmental correlations were large, which suggests continuity. The effects of shared environment were significant for the MDI at 20 and 24 months, and the R_c is 1.0, indicating that a common environmental effect across this age span is highly likely. Finally, the age-to-age correlations for unique environment were relatively low for the MDI and all other variables, suggesting a lack of continuity over time for this source of variance.

Modeling Continuity and Change

Large age-to-age variance correlations imply continuity across age but do not reveal whether a particular influence contributes to phenotypic similarity. Small age-to-age variance correlations may imply the presence of change (i.e., new influences emerging at each age), or they may indicate a lack of any

81

systematic influence on cross-age variance. Finally, this bivariate perspective cannot identify continuity and change across three ages. A more powerful technique is needed to examine these possibilities.

We used the *Cholesky decomposition* (also called a *triangular factorization*) to explore the extent to which genetic or environmental effects account for the same variance across age or introduce new variance at each assessment (for additional details, see Cherny, Fulker, Emde, et al., 1994; Fulker et al., 1993; Loehlin, 1996; Neale & Cardon, 1992). In the present context of three assessment ages, the Cholesky decomposition provides a model with weightings for six parameters organized into three factors: a factor with parameters at 14, 20, and 24 months; a factor with parameters at 20 and 24 months; and a factor with a single parameter at 24 months.

The weights for these six parameters can be interpreted as follows. A model that has a single factor with significant weights at 14, 20, and 24 months suggests a source of variation that is present at Time 1 but that also contributes to subsequent time points. Figure 3*a* is a graphic presentation of a model with a single factor (labeled F1) that accounts for continuity in phenotypic variance across three ages (labeled P14, P20, and P24). A model in which significant parameters emerge for each of several factors suggests the presence of age-specific sources of variation. Figure 3*b* portrays a model with significant parameters for factor 1 at 14 months, factor 2 at 20 months, and factor 3 at 24 months. This model suggests change in the sense that a new factor emerges to account for variance at each age. Other patterns of parameters suggest other interpretations. For example, Figure 3*c* suggests both continuity and change: factor 1 accounts for variance at 14, 20, and 24 months, factor 2 accounts for change at 20 months but promotes continuity to 24 months, and factor 3 accounts for change at 24 months. Finally, Figure 3*d* is also a model of continuity and change, but, in this case, factor 1 accounts for continuity across ages 14, 20, and 24 months, and a second factor accounts for change at 24 months.

As applied to twin data, the full Cholesky model consists of separate decompositions (i.e., sets of factors like those described earlier) for each of three variance components: genetic, shared environmental, and unique environmental. Consider a genetic interpretation of the first two factor patterns described earlier: A model with a factor that is common to all three time points suggests genetic continuity (i.e., a single genetic effect that persists over time). A model in which new factors exert influence at each age suggests

FIGURE 3.—Graphic representation of a hypothetical Cholesky decomposition. *a,* A single factor accounts for continuity across three ages. *b,* A factor is present at each age, thus suggesting change. *c,* One factor accounts for continuity across ages. A second factor is associated with change at 20 months and then continuity to 24 months. *d,* One factor accounts for continuity across ages. A second factor is associated with change at 24 months.

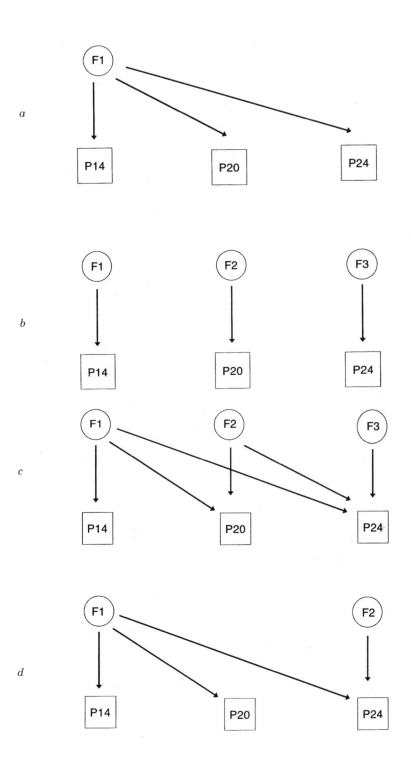

genetic change (i.e., a new genetic effect emerges at each time point). Comparable explanations could be provided for these two models if the factor pattern referred to shared or unique environment.

The first step in a Cholesky decomposition is the calculation of weights for a full model (i.e., a model with 18 parameters: six each for the heritability, shared environment, and unique environment parameters). A variety of optimization software packages are available to estimate the factor loadings from twin data classified as MZ and DZ, but general purpose structural equation modeling programs such as LISREL (Joreskog & Sorbom, 1989) necessitate the elimination of data from any twin pairs not measured at all time points. To make maximal use of the data, we estimated factor loadings with PEDIKID (Cardon, 1991), which uses a maximum-likelihood pedigree approach in which the model is fit to observed data rather than covariance matrices. Comparable results can be obtained through the more widely known MX program (Neale, 1994). The approach used in this study assumes that data are missing at random, which is a reasonable assumption for the present variables given the failure in the previous analyses to find differences in comparisons between the incomplete data set and a set that includes only families with complete data.

There are also various techniques for determining the most parsimonious model that adequately accounts for the observed cross-twin and cross-time cross-twin resemblance for each measure. We began the model-fitting process by calculating a full model in which three factors are included for all three types of variance (i.e., there are 18 parameters). This model offers the best fit to the data by definition in the sense that no factors can be added to account for any additional variance. From this starting point, the usefulness of various parameters in the model can be evaluated through an iterative process of model testing in which we remove a parameter or a set of parameters and determine the extent to which the reduced model still fits the data. If the parameter can be removed without adversely affecting the fit between the model and the data, then we assume that there is justification for removing that parameter from the model. If the fit becomes significantly worse, this suggests that the parameter in question is an important aspect of the model and should be retained. The change in fit between two models can be compared by doubling the difference between the negative log likelihoods for the models, which is asymptotically distributed as chi square.

Note that the implicit goal here is parsimony as formally defined by the Akaike Information Criterion (AIC; Akaike, 1987), in which a 1 degree of freedom change is tolerable if it results in a worsening of the model's fit by a chi square no greater than 2. Other goodness-of-fit indices have been proposed to assess the statistical adequacy of the fitted model compared with a null model (Tanaka, 1993). However, we will limit our discussion to the AIC, which has a straightforward interpretation and has proved useful across a variety of contexts (Williams & Holohan, 1994). Note that the parsimonious model must still offer an adequate accounting for the variance in the data.

When a parameter has been removed from the model, the weights of the other parameters can change. This change in weights occurs because the reduced model makes new variance available for other parameters to claim. There are two implications of this fact. First, the initial pattern of weights provided by the full model provides a tentative view of the parameters that should be relevant (i.e., relevant parameters will have higher weights), but the initial pattern may be misleading. Subsequent changes in the model can cause drastic changes in the pattern of weights. For example, a strong first parameter can make a potentially useful second or third parameter unnecessary. Or an entire source of variance that contains nonzero weights may be eliminated with no adverse effect on the model's fit. This implies the need for caution in interpreting weights from the full model. Second, the particular order in which parameters are removed from the model can affect which model emerges as the most parsimonious. This implies the need for a theoretical rationale to guide the process of model evaluation (i.e., to determine which parameters should be tested for elimination first).

Table 15 lists the loadings from the full model for each of six parameters within each of three partitions of variance (i.e., genetic, shared environment, and nonshared environment). The parameters in bold are those that are retained in the final model and that have values that will be reestimated (as will be described later), but we will first examine the general pattern across the full models. The most consistent pattern of loadings across measures is the age-related change for unique environment: for all variables, the variance for unique environment is associated with large values on the diagonal of the matrix (i.e., for factor 1 at 14 months, factor 2 at 20 months, and factor 3 at 24 months). This effect could be interpreted as reflecting dramatic change in the unique environment at each age, but note that measurement error is indistinguishable from unique environmental influences that act on a certain measure at a certain time (i.e., unique environment and error of measurement are both reasons why MZ twins do not have the same score). In either case, because of the consistent age-specific effect of unique environment across variables, our first step in each model was to remove the three parameters associated with continuity of unique environment (i.e., the parameters not on the diagonal: the two parameters in factor 1 that are associated with 20 and 24 months and the one parameter in factor 2 that is associated with 24 months). As expected, the loss of these parameters did not adversely affect the fit for any variable. The search for a parsimonious model was well launched.

Before we describe the subsequent steps in the iterative process of model testing, it will be useful to introduce a technique for representing the models graphically. Figure 4 is the final model for change and continuity in MDI

TABLE 15

Standardized Loadings from the Full Model

	Category of Variance								
	Genetic			Shared Environment			Unique Environment		
Variable and Age	Factor 1	Factor 2	Factor 3	Factor 1	Factor 2	Factor 3	Factor 1	Factor 2	Factor 3
BSID MDI:									
14 months	**.64**			**.43**	.44		**.64**		
20 months	**.33**	.47		**.54**			.05	**.43**	
24 months	**.31**	.29	.46	**.51**	.42	.00	.03	.03	**.41**
Nonverbal:									
14 months	**.64**			.27			**.68**		
20 months	**.40**	**.70**		.32	.00		.04	**.61**	
24 months	**.32**	**.59**	**.61**	.45	.00	.00	.06	.02	**.58**
Verbal expressive:									
14 months	.30			**.55**			**.60**		
20 months	.13	**.49**		**.53**	**.47**		.00	**.56**	
24 months	.27	**.31**	.20	**.49**	**.34**	**.45**	.04	.01	**.53**
Verbal receptive:									
14 months	**.54**			**.59**			**.68**		
20 months	**.27**	.34		**.50**	**.50**		.00	**.54**	
24 months	**.15**	.43	.00	**.49**	**.41**	**-.32**	.07	.03	**.58**
Word comprehension:									
14 months	.05			**.33**			**.94**		
20 months	-.20	.00		**.47**	-.11		.01	**.85**	
24 months	-.35	.00	.00	**.29**	-.24	.00	.00	.03	**.86**
Visual attention:									
14 months	**.59**			**.43**			**.68**		
20 months	**.53**	.53		**.22**	**.25**		.11	**.57**	
24 months	**.28**	.62	.00	**.20**	**.34**	.00	.03	.04	**.62**
Memory for locations:									
14 months	.42			**.29**			**.86**		
20 months	.13	**.46**		**.20**	**.02**		.06	**.86**	
24 months	.06	**.41**	.00	.14	**.02**	.00	.02	.03	**.90**

Note.—Boldface indicates factor loading that was retained in the most parsimonious model.

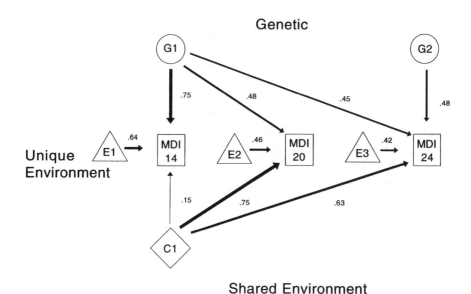

FIGURE 4.—Final model for continuity and change in MDI scores

scores. Phenotypic variance in MDI at each time point is represented by squares labeled MDI14, MDI20, and MDI24. At this point in the modeling process, we have established that nonshared environment (represented by the triangles labeled E1, E2, and E3) accounts for change in phenotypic variance at each point in time. The arrows in Figure 4 between E1 and MDI14, between E2 and MDI20, and between E3 and MDI24 indicate the presence of a significant parameter (i.e., significant in the sense that it cannot be removed without adversely affecting the model's fit). The number beside each arrow indicates the strength of the effect (i.e., the weight of that parameter), and the arrow shafts are drawn with widths proportional to the strength of the effect.

Returning now to the theme of unique environment, the arrows between the triangles and the squares at each assessment age in Figures 5–10 indicate that unique environment affected change in all variables measured here. Effects were smaller for the MDI than for the components, but this probably reflects the increase in error that occurs when fewer items are used as a basis for measurement. Effects of unique environment were particularly high for the laboratory procedures.

We next focus on the genetic parameters. For each model, we first attempted to remove all six genetic parameters (i.e., tested the hypothesis that there was no genetic influence on change or continuity). This step reduced the fit for all variables except word comprehension and memory for locations.

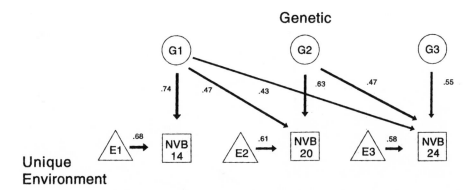

FIGURE 5.—Final model for continuity and change in nonverbal scores

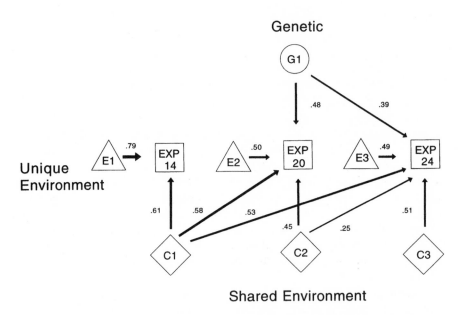

FIGURE 6.—Final model for continuity and change in expressive language scores

As indicated in Figures 8 and 10, the final models for these variables contain no genetic influences.[13] To discover the appropriate genetic parameters for the other variables, we first explored (i.e., attempted to remove) an effect of

[13] Eliminating parameters in a different order (as in Wilson, Corley, Fulker, & Reznick, 1996) can strengthen the case for genetic influences on memory for locations, which is compatible with the weak genetic effects that emerge for univariate analyses at 14 and 20 months.

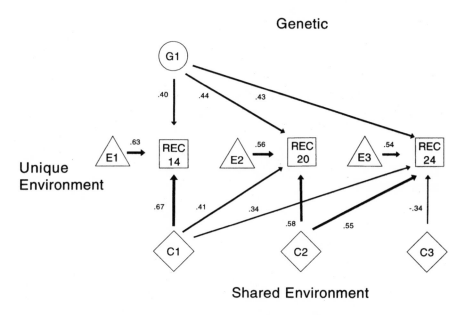

FIGURE 7.—Final model for continuity and change in receptive language scores

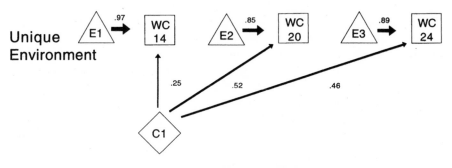

FIGURE 8.—Final model for continuity and change in word-comprehension scores

genetic continuity (as in Figure 3*a* above) and an effect of genetic change (as in Figure 3*b* above). On the basis of the results of these models and the resultant parameter weights, we attempted to remove other parameters until the most parsimonious model was discovered. These genetic effects are represented in Figures 4–10 as arrows from the circles labeled G1, G2, and G3.[14]

---

[14] The column headings in Table 15 and in Table 20 below indicate factor numbers in a categorical rather than an ordinal sense. For example, in Table 15, the genetic effects on

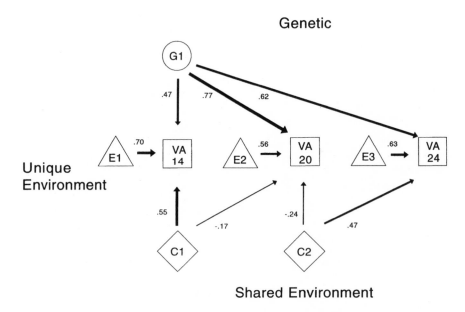

FIGURE 9.—Final model for continuity and change in visual attention scores

The model of the MDI (Figure 4) suggested genetic continuity across the three assessment ages (with particularly strong influence at 14 months) but also the emergence of new genetic variance at 24 months. The models for the components offer additional resolution. For the score based on non-verbal items (Figure 5), there was a genetic effect promoting continuity, an additional genetic effect that promoted change at 20 months but continuity through 24 months, and a third genetic effect that accounted for change at 24 months. For the language measures, a genetic effect promoted continuity between 20 and 24 months for expressive language (Figure 6) and between 14 and 24 months for receptive language (Figure 7). From this perspective, one interpretation of the genetic change at 24 months for the MDI is that an additional parameter becomes necessary to account for expressive language. There were no genetic effects on change or continuity for the laboratory measures of word comprehension (Figure 8) and memory for locations (Figure 10), which is compatible with their marginal age-specific genetic effects (Table 12 above) and weak cross-time phenotypic continuity. The genetic influ-

the MDI can be partitioned into a factor that promotes continuity (i.e., has significant influence at 14, 20, and 24 months) and a factor that promotes change (i.e., has an effect at 24 months only). The change factor is represented as factor 3 in the table owing to the particular column in which it is represented but as factor G2 in Figure 4 because it is the second relevant genetic factor.

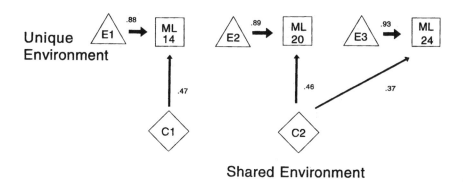

Shared Environment

FIGURE 10.—Final model for continuity and change in memory for locations scores

ence on visual attentiveness was accounted for by a single factor promoting continuity from 14 months (Figure 9).

We next used the same model selection procedure for the shared environment parameters: we first tested a model suggesting no effect of shared environment. The model with no effect of shared environment was retained for the nonverbal construct only, which is not surprising given the minimal influence of c^2 on age-specific analyses of the nonverbal construct. The remaining variables were explored with models of continuity and change, and individual parameters were tested until the most parsimonious model emerged. The parameters associated with shared environment are represented as arrows from the diamonds labeled C1, C2, and C3 in Figures 4–10.

The model for MDI revealed that shared environment affected continuity, but the weight of this effect was small at 14 months. Interestingly, when the MDI was recast as separate constructs, there was no effect of shared environment at all for the nonverbal questions, but shared environment affected continuity and change in both measures of language. This pattern is compatible with the age-specific effects. Shared environment promoted continuity across age for the laboratory measure of word comprehension and contiguous age continuity for visual attentiveness. The pattern of weights for visual attentiveness contained two negative parameters, which suggested change in the valence of a particular influence, but absolute values were small, and age-specific effects were low, undermining the significance of this result. Finally, shared environment had a transitory effect on memory for locations at 14 months and a more persistent effect (promoting change in memory) that emerged at 20 months and remained stable through 24 months. This, too, must be interpreted in the context of trivial age-specific effects and the decision to eliminate any genetic influences on either continuity or change prior to fitting shared environmental parameters.

TABLE 16

Correspondence of Various Indices of Quantitative Developmental Function for MZ
and DZ Twin Pairs and Modeled Effects of Heredity and Shared Environment

Index and Measure	MZ	DZ	MZ vs. DZ	h^2	c^2
Pattern:					
Nonverbal	.28	.20	. . .	. . .	. . .
	(85)	(63)			
Expressive	.45*	.33*	. . .	. . .	. . .
	(131)	(124)			
Receptive	.26*	.26	. . .	. . .	. . .
	(148)	(128)			
Linear coefficient:					
Nonverbal	.51**	.22**	2.92*	.49*	.00
	(163)	(139)		[.06]	
Expressive	.52**	.30**	2.35*	.43*	.07
	(167)	(144)		[.21]	[.18]
Receptive	.50**	.35**	1.58	.31	.19
	(169)	(147)		[.20]	[.16]
Range:					
Nonverbal	.59**	.39**	2.63**	.41*	.18
	(210)	(177)		[.18]	[.15]
Expressive	.78**	.54**	4.76**	.49*	.29*
	(210)	(177)		[.15]	[.12]
Receptive	.75**	.62**	2.53*	.27*	.48*
	(210)	(177)		[.15]	[.12]

Note.—Statistical tests for correlations are one tailed. Degrees of freedom are given in parentheses. Comparison of MZ vs. DZ correlations is based on one-tailed z scores. Statistical tests for h^2 and c^2 are one tailed. A parameter of .00 indicates use of constrained model. Standard errors corrected for double entry are given in brackets.

* $p < .05$.
** $p < .01$.

QUANTITATIVE DEVELOPMENTAL FUNCTION

To determine the similarity of twin pairs on quantitative developmental function, we calculated contingency coefficients to measure the strength of the association between assignments into the categories of change designated *early, continuous,* and *late.* The values of the contingency coefficient for MZ and DZ pairs for each construct are listed in Table 16. The magnitude of the contingency coefficient reflects the extent to which twins tended to be classified into the same quantitative developmental function. Contingency coefficients are affected by the number of categories (i.e., possible developmental functions), but, for the measures used in this study, the numbers of categories are equal. For the nonverbal and expressive language constructs, MZ and DZ twins had some degree of association, but the MZ values were larger, which suggests modest effects of genetics and shared environment. The absolute values of the coefficients were larger for expressive language, which could indicate less effect of unique environment. For receptive language, MZ and

TABLE 17

CORRESPONDENCE FOR VARIOUS INDICES OF
QUALITATIVE DEVELOPMENTAL FUNCTIONS

Index and Age	MZ	DZ
Nonverbal vs. verbal:		
14 months	.15*	.02
	(205)	(173)
20 months	.52**	.01
	(183)	(159)
24 months	.33**	.13
	(180)	(158)
Expressive vs. receptive:		
14 months	.23*	.00
	(203)	(173)
20 months	.49**	.27*
	(180)	(152)
24 months	.09	.25*
	(179)	(154)

NOTE.—Correlation values are based on phi coefficients. Degrees of freedom are given in parentheses.
  * $p < .05$.
  ** $p < .01$.

DZ coefficients were identical, suggesting an effect of shared environment but no genetic influence.

Additional analyses of quantitative developmental function were calculated for the linear coefficients. The ordinal level of measurement for this variable allowed us to use Pearson correlations and the DeFries and Fulker model. As indicated in Table 16, MZ-DZ differences were significant for the nonverbal and expressive measures and marginally different for the receptive measure, suggesting genetic effects. The DeFries and Fulker model indicated heritability for the nonverbal and expressive measures. The pattern for receptive language was similar to the pattern for expressive language, but the effect of heritability was smaller, and the effect of shared environment was larger. The pattern of effects for range (an additional aspect of quantitative developmental function) indicated significant genetic effects for all variables and effects of shared environment for both measures of language.

QUALITATIVE DEVELOPMENTAL FUNCTION

Genetic and environmental effects for qualitative developmental function were estimated by comparing the cross-classifications of MZ and DZ twins on the basis of their relative performance on nonverbal and verbal questions. This dichotomous partition into verbal and nonverbal allowed us to calculate the phi coefficient as a measure of association for the cross-classification of

TABLE 18

Twin Intraclass Correlations and Estimates of Genetic (h^2) and Shared Environmental (c^2) Variance for the Difference between Expressive and Receptive Scores

Age	MZ	DZ	h^2	c^2
14 months	.23**	.03	.20*	.00
	(205)	(173)	[.06]	
20 months	.26**	.15**	.23	.03
	(181)	(158)	[.21]	[.18]
24 months	.33**	.34**	.00	.33**
	(180)	(156)		[.05]

Note.—Statistical tests for correlations are one tailed. Degrees of freedom are given in parentheses. Statistical tests for h^2 and c^2 are one tailed. A parameter of .00 indicates use of constrained model. Standard errors corrected for double entry are given in brackets.

* $p < .05$.

** $p < .01$.

MZ and DZ twins. As indicated in Table 17, MZ coefficients were statistically significant and seemed larger than DZ coefficients at each age, but the effect was strongest at 20 months. The raw values at 20 months underscore this claim: 83 DZ twin pairs were classified the same (i.e., both verbal or both nonverbal), and 69 DZ twin pairs were mixed. For MZ twins, 141 twin pairs were classified the same, and only 39 were mixed.

We also explored each child's classification as either expressive or receptive on the basis of which of these two measures was larger. As indicated in Table 17, MZ coefficients were statistically significant at 14 and 20 months and tended to be larger than DZ correlations, suggesting a genetic effect. The MZ correlations at 24 months were abnormally low: 46% of MZ twin pairs were discrepant (i.e., one had a higher score on the expressive measure, the other on the receptive measure), as opposed to 37% of DZ twin pairs. These results suggest a genetic influence on relative performance on nonverbal measures but an environmental influence on the aspect of language that is most prominent.

Finally, we calculated the absolute difference between expressive and receptive language scores, which is one metric of correspondence between these two domains of the lexicon. As indicated in Table 18, both MZ and DZ correlations were significant at 24 months, suggesting an effect of shared environment, and MZ-DZ differences were notable at 14 and 20 months, suggesting a heritable influence. The DeFries and Fulker analysis confirms these observations: there is a significant effect of h^2 at 14 months and a significant effect of c^2 at 24 months. The effect of h^2 at 20 months is relatively large but not statistically significant. This pattern of effects suggests genetic influence on the relation between expressive and receptive language early in the second year but an environmental effect that emerges as language becomes more sophisticated.

TABLE 19

Implied Matrix of Genetic (R_g), Shared Environment (R_c), and Unique Environment (R_e) Correlations for Cross-Measure Comparisons at Each Age

Age and Variable	Genetic (R_g)		Shared Environment (R_c)		Unique Environment (R_e)	
	Receptive	Nonverbal	Receptive	Nonverbal	Receptive	Nonverbal
14 months:						
Expressive	-.00	-.18	.99	.99	.23	.34
Receptive		.38		.92		.24
20 months:						
Expressive	.77	-.03	.72	.88	.35	.12
Receptive		-.11		.97		.25
24 months:						
Expressive	.82	.61	.80	.75	.22	-.02
Receptive		.89		.82		-.07

TABLE 20

Standardized Loadings from the Full Model across Nonverbal, Expressive, and Receptive Constructs at Each Age

| | Category of Variance | | | | | | | | |
| | Genetic | | | Shared Environment | | | Unique Environment | | |
Age and Variable	Factor 1	Factor 2	Factor 3	Factor 1	Factor 2	Factor 3	Factor 1	Factor 2	Factor 3
14 months:									
Nonverbal	**.64**			**.31**			**.70**		
Expressive	−.05	**.27**		**.55**	.15		**.26**	**.73**	
Receptive	**.20**	.03	**.50**	**.55**	.23	.00	.15	.09	**.58**
20 months:									
Nonverbal	**.54**			**.56**			**.63**		
Expressive	−.02	**.51**		**.62**	.34		.06	**.49**	
Receptive	−.04	**.25**	.21	**.73**	−.19	.00	.14	.19	**.52**
24 months:									
Nonverbal	**.72**			**.40**			**.57**		
Expressive	**.29**	**.38**		**.55**	.49		.00	**.48**	
Receptive	**.39**	.15	.12	**.60**	.19	.36	−.04	.12	**.52**

Note.—Boldface indicates factor loading that was retained in the most parsimonious model.

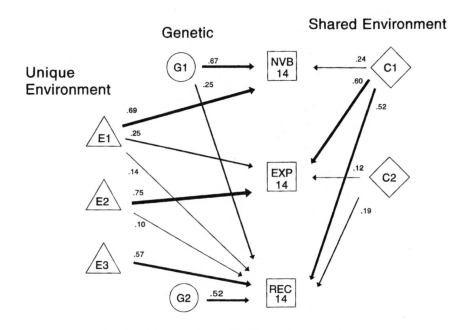

FIGURE 11.—Final model for overlap and distinctiveness in nonverbal, expressive language, and receptive language scores at 14 months.

OVERLAP AND DISTINCTIVENESS ACROSS MEASURES

The approach to continuity and change across time presented in the previous section can be applied to overlap and distinctiveness across measures as well. That is, for each assessment age, we can explore whether genetic, shared environmental, and unique environmental influences accounted for shared variance (overlap) or promoted change (distinctiveness) across measures. This question is relevant only for measures that do not share items. Furthermore, although a model could be calculated across any number of variables at a particular age, a large model would be extremely complex and of relatively low power. To avoid overlap due to shared items, and to maintain parallel structure with the models that contained three ages, we limited the models under discussion here to three variables: the nonverbal measure, the expressive measure, and the receptive measure. These variables seemed reasonably parallel and were the most "well behaved" in the analyses reported earlier. Moreover, their combination in a single analysis allowed us to explore theoretically interesting questions about the relation between nonverbal and linguistic measures of intelligence and the relation between expressive and receptive aspects of language.

As in the previous section, the first step was to inspect the separate cross-

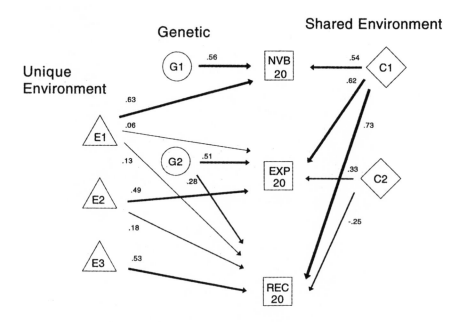

FIGURE 12.—Final model for overlap and distinctiveness in nonverbal, expressive language, and receptive language scores at 20 months.

measure correlations for genetic variance (R_g), shared environmental variance (R_c), and unique environmental variance (R_e) at each age in the context of significant effects of h^2 and c^2. These correlations, presented in Table 19, are useful because they indicate whether the variance that can be attributed to a specific influence was shared between pairs of outcome variables. There was genetic overlap at 14 months between nonverbal and receptive constructs, at 20 months between expressive and receptive constructs, and at 24 months among all three constructs. Overlap for shared environment was high across all measures at each age. Finally, there appeared to be some overlap in unique environment across all three measures at 14 and 20 months and across the measures of language at 24 months.

We then calculated Cholesky models using the technique described earlier, but here the factors refer to effects across variables rather than effects across ages. The choice of an order of entry for measures collected at the same time is arbitrary in comparison with the age-based ordering that is obvious for longitudinal measures. In the present analysis, we entered the nonverbal measure first, followed by the expressive measure, then the receptive measure. Loehlin (1996) has argued that alternative models of the relation between variables collected at the same time may be more informative than the Cholesky decomposition, with the latter being regarded as a starting place

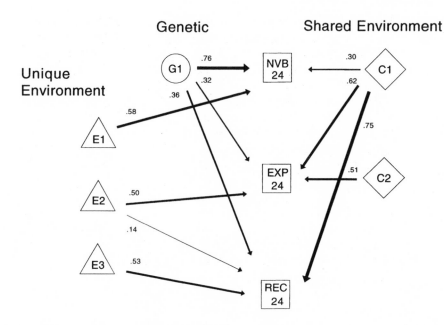

FIGURE 13.—Final model for overlap and distinctiveness in nonverbal, expressive language, and receptive language scores at 24 months.

for additional transformations. However, in the absence of a strong a priori basis for preferring one of several alternative models, the Cholesky decomposition provides a useful tool for assessing the genetic and environmental correlations of multiple measures collected at the same time.

Table 20 shows the parameters for the full model in bold to indicate parameters retained in the final model. The values for the parameters in the final model are shown in Figures 11–13. The effect of unique environment was distinct (i.e., specific to each measure), but there was also some overlap across measures, in contrast with the cross-time models. The most parsimonious model included some overlapping paths at each age, but there was less overlap at successive ages. The strongest effects of unique environment were distinct influences on each measure.

The most parsimonious model of genetic influence at 14 months suggested a single genetic factor that influenced the nonverbal measure, with some overlap to the receptive construct and a distinct genetic influence on receptive language. At 20 months, there was a genetic influence on the nonverbal construct and a distinct genetic influence that affected both measures of language. However, at 24 months, a single genetic effect was most strongly associated with the nonverbal construct but also promoted overlap across the language constructs.

For shared environment, the parsimonious model at 14 months indicated strong overlap for the language measures and some overlap to the nonverbal measure. A second source accounted for additional slight overlap in language. The pattern at 20 months was similar, but the overlap was stronger among the three measures. There was also a curious second parameter that affected both measures of language but that had different signs for the expressive and receptive constructs. The pattern at 24 months indicated a general overlap among measures that was strongest for language and a second influence specific to expressive language.

XIII. BRIEF SUMMARY OF RESULTS

RELATIONS AMONG DEPENDENT VARIABLES

The dependent variables tended to be intercorrelated, but word comprehension, visual attention, and memory for locations were relatively independent. Intercorrelations among most variables increased from 14 to 20 months. Receptive items accounted for the largest portion of variance in the MDI at each age and across ages. In a comparison of relative performance on the nonverbal, expressive, and receptive measures, infants scored higher on verbal items at each age.

GROUP DIFFERENCES

MDI scores for twins were relatively normal. Average scores on each measure increased across the second year, but contiguous ages were comparable for some measures. Females had higher scores than males on most measures; these differences tended to be larger at 20 and 24 months.

Most infants who had some degree of change in the nonverbal measure over time had their greatest change between 20 and 24 months. Most infants who had change in the language measures had their greatest change between 14 and 20 months. In a comparison of receptive and expressive language, receptive language was more likely to change in the early interval, and expressive language was more likely to change in the late interval.

INDIVIDUAL DIFFERENCES

Birth weight was positively correlated with MDI. There was a weak but significant relation between assessment age (within an age bracket) and most outcome measures. Parents' education was positively correlated with infants' performance on most measures from 14 months. The relation was stronger at 24 months. The physical similarity of DZ twins had no effect on any variable except for memory for locations at 14 months. Most measures were less stable across the interval from 14 to 20 months than across the interval from 20 to 24 months. Infants tended to have similar patterns of developmental change across variables.

GENETIC AND ENVIRONMENTAL INFLUENCES

There were significant effects of h^2 on the MDI at each assessment and effects of c^2 at 20 and 24 months, but this pattern differed for specific components: There were effects of h^2 for the nonverbal measures at each assessment but no effects of c^2; expressive language had effects of c^2 at each assessment, with effects of h^2 emerging at 20 and 24 months; receptive language had effects of c^2 at each age, with negligible effects of h^2 after 14 months. There were strong effects of e^2 on each variable at each age.

For most measures, there were stronger genetic effects for males and shared environment effects for females at 14 and 20 months. Statistical support for this conclusion was weak.

Genetic effects on the MDI accounted for the same variance across age (continuity) and for unique variance at 24 months (change). Shared environment effects on the MDI accounted for continuity across age. From the perspective of specific measures, genetic influences on the nonverbal measure accounted for continuity across age and change at each age, but shared environment had no influence. Genetic influences accounted for continuity across age on expressive and receptive language measures. The influence of shared environment on expressive and receptive language accounted for continuity across age and change at each age. Shared environment accounted for continuity in word comprehension across age, continuity in memory for locations from 20 to 24 months, and continuity in visual attentiveness from 14 to 20 months and from 20 to 24 months. There was also a genetic influence promoting continuity in visual attentiveness across age. Unique environment accounted for change in each measure at each age.

The pattern of results for genetic and environmental effects on quantitative and qualitative developmental function was complex. Various indices of change in nonverbal and expressive scores suggested genetic effects with some environmental influence. Change in receptive language suggested a stronger effect of environment. The performance of infants on nonverbal relative to verbal items seemed strongly heritable. Performance on expressive relative to receptive items was heritable at 14 and 20 months but affected by shared environment at 24 months. A comparable pattern emerged for absolute difference in expressive and receptive scores.

A formal comparison of the influences on nonverbal, expressive, and receptive measures at each age revealed a complex pattern of effects. Genetic influences promoted overlap between nonverbal and receptive measures at 14 months, between expressive and receptive measures at 20 months, and among all three measures at 24 months. Shared environment promoted overlap among measures at each assessment but also had a distinct influence on the two language measures. Unique environment tended to influence each measure separately at each age.

XIV. LIMITATIONS ON GENERALIZATIONS

Our main goal in this *Monograph* is to learn more about the development of intelligence in the second year, with intelligence defined as a general capacity or as a set of separable abilities. Several aspects of this phenomenon have been explored. Before specific results are discussed, it is prudent to describe some limitations affecting interpretation of the results reported here.

SAMPLE CHARACTERISTICS

The generalizations that can be derived from psychological research on any sample are limited. The sample reported here is essentially homogeneous for race and culture, reflecting a predominantly European-American, English-speaking, well-educated, middle- and upper-middle-class population. These constraints limit generalizations to a broader, multicultural population. Moreover, the children in this sample are twins, which may limit generalizations to nontwin populations. Twins tend to have lower birth weights than singletons, but the twins recruited for this study were selected to be heavier. The main advantage of this strategy is that our results can be generalized to the broader population of children with normal birth weights. However, one disadvantage is that our results may not generalize to twins who are normal in the sense of having relatively low birth weights. This unique aspect of the present sample may explain some discrepancies between our results and the results reported for traditional twin studies (e.g., the Louisville Twin Study).

A more general question is whether twins and their families are fundamentally different from singletons and their families. In some sense, the answer to this question must be yes, for the presence of a same-aged companion surely affects many aspects of a child's daily life. Further, the challenge of caring for two same-aged children must evoke some stress in families, materially as well as psychologically. Although these facts suggest the need for caution in generalizing from the findings presented in this *Monograph,* the problem is offset somewhat given that the cognitive processes investigated here are fundamental human abilities that develop normally in most twins. The data reported here show no indication that twins with normal birth weights have systematic retardation of intelligence. Indeed, Bayley MDI scores, which are widely considered to be a measure of general intelligence, are above normal in the present sample, and the lowest-scoring twins are within the normal range. Twins are born small and accrue associated risks, but we find no evidence that twins with normal birth weights can be distinguished from singletons by their intellectual capacity. Thus, we believe that the results reported here address aspects of normal development.

DEPENDENT VARIABLES

Our effort to partition infant intelligence (particularly as measured by the MDI) into specific constructs was successful. In some sense, the proof is in the bounty of findings summarized in the following chapters, but, from a methodological perspective, the constructs met acceptable standards.

We attempted to capture the rich complexity of language with two parameters drawn from observations in limited contexts. This approach is obviously incomplete: It focuses on the lexicon rather than on syntax. It is primarily concerned with nominals rather than with other word classes. It is explicitly about monolingual speakers of English. And it ignores other techniques for assessing early language (e.g., parents' diary records of new words, observation of linguistic behavior, and physiological response to linguistic stimuli).

The present variables do, however, have merit. The distinction between expressive and receptive domains is particularly relevant for describing the lexicon as it emerges in the second year, and it has implications for verbal ability in older children and adults as well (Sincoff & Sternberg, 1987). The index of expressive language used in this study was derived on the basis of infants' spontaneous comments and of speech that could be evoked in various contexts in the laboratory and the home. This measure is related to word knowledge, but it also taps discourse ability and talkativeness. The index of receptive language was derived on the basis not only of the children's response to questions, thus reflecting knowledge of word reference, but also of the children's compliance with a request to point to, hand over, or look at a particular stimulus.

The two language variables were internally consistent and externally valid: there was significant agreement across the various questions about language and between observer report and parent report. Also, for receptive language, there was agreement between observer report and the laboratory-based word-comprehension test. The usefulness of the latter procedure was potentially limited by our decision to use age-appropriate stimuli, the artificial nature of those stimuli, and peculiarities of the laboratory context. However,

105

the congruence of conclusions made on the basis of the referential language construct and the word-comprehension scores suggests the relative impotence of these threats to validity. The measures of expressive and receptive language were correlated, which is expected given their shared base of representational processes and lexical knowledge, but considerable variance was available to reflect other processes.

A strong case emerged against the use of SICD questions derived from parent report of twin language as a means for assessing the language accomplishments of individual twins. Parent report of twin language indicates considerably more twin similarity than does observer report of twin language. Parents have ample opportunity to observe child language, and it is well established that parents can provide rich and accurate information regarding their child's expressive and receptive competence (e.g., Fenson et al., 1993; Reznick & Goldfield, 1994). However, the extremely large MZ and DZ twin correlations for the parent-report scores are problematic, for they suggest that, despite good information and the best intentions, parents have difficulty distinguishing between the language accomplishments of their two twins, at least as assessed by using the SICD. It is not surprising that accuracy would be particularly compromised when parents are attempting to report on younger twins, whose vocabulary is limited and often unstable. Alternatively, the large parent-report twin correlations could reflect the more general phenomenon that multiple ratings provided by an individual observer (particularly an untrained observer) are not independent. At least, parents do not seem compelled to establish a notable contrast for DZ twins, which can be problematic for parent report of dimensions of temperament (e.g., for apparent contrast effects in the present sample's scores on the Colorado Childhood Temperament Inventory, see Plomin et al., 1993). Because of these concerns, we dropped parent-report items from the expressive and receptive language constructs.

The nonverbal abilities tapped in the BSID are obviously different from nonverbal aspects of intelligence in adults, but they do capture a range of nonverbal skills that infants acquire or perfect during the second year, including fine motor coordination, the ability to imitate, and the ability to use a means-end strategy to solve simple problems. The nonverbal items have strong internal consistency. However, this construct was not highly correlated with the other nonverbal measures. Additional work will be needed to establish the cohesiveness and most appropriate definition of the nonverbal construct, but it seems similar to the factors that Lewis et al. (1986) labeled *means-end, imitation,* and *spatial.* The nonverbal construct spans a range of different abilities, yet it is more specific than the construct entailed by the MDI score. For present purposes, it offers a useful parallel comparison with the expressive and receptive constructs.

Attention is a broad concept reflecting multisensory orientation in the service of information gathering and information processing. We measured visual attention rather than orientation per se and conducted this measurement in the limited context of the word-comprehension procedure. Despite these limitations, the measure of visual attention used in this study seems to be tapping a significant aspect of the infant's nonverbal ability. Visual attention was not highly correlated with nonverbal ability at 14 months, but the relation became stronger at later assessments. More important, visual attention and nonverbal ability showed similar patterns of heritable and environmental effects.

It seems reasonable to expect that change in memory ability during the second year affects the infant's intellectual ability, but the memory for locations test used in this study was relatively unsuccessful. Correlations were low between memory for locations and other variables and between twins' memory scores and their parents' education. Cross-time correlations for memory for locations were lower than for any other measure.

The pattern of effects for twin comparisons is intriguing, but it must be interpreted with caution. The obvious problems with the memory for locations task are the lack of precision (there are only 11 steps on the scale) and the lack of an iterative process to establish a basal level and a ceiling of ability. An additional problem is that some children reach a ceiling of performance on the memory for locations task (i.e., solve the task at the longest delay), thus precluding accurate assessment of their memory ability. Moreover, the ceiling effect increases with age: 1%, 7%, and 14% of children at 14, 20, and 24 months, respectively, passed the test at the highest level of performance.

Note that performance on the memory for locations task was probably affected by other cognitive competences. For example, previous research indicates that performance in a memory for locations task reflects both memory and the ability to inhibit a prepotent motor response (Diamond, 1990; Hofstadter & Reznick, 1996). Also, the interactive nature of the memory for locations task causes it to tap various emotional domains, such as the infant's willingness to release the object so that the experimenter can hide it again and frustration when search is incorrect.

Although this measurement of memory is problematic, it is likely that whatever ability it taps could be considered nonverbal (i.e., the child does not need to understand language to perform the task). Note that the memory for locations task is derived from procedures often used with nonhuman primates who have not been exposed to human speech.

TWIN ANALYSIS MODELS

The estimation of effects in the twin analysis model requires various assumptions, some of which are difficult to confirm. For example, the estimate of heritability calculated by doubling the difference between MZ and DZ correlations assumes that the genetic effect of sharing 100% of genes is twice the effect of sharing, on average, 50% of genes. MZ twins have identical structural genotypes, but genetic regulating mechanisms can alter the functional genotype that is present at any point in time (Goldsmith, 1993) and thus introduce variance into cross-age comparisons. If genetic effects are not additive, DZ twins are less than half as similar as MZ twins, and the MZ-DZ difference overestimates the genetic effect.

In the analyses reported here, constrained model-fitting procedures have been used that limit heritability to a value not exceeding the MZ correlation, which prevents grievous overestimates of genetic effects but does not prevent some error if genetic variance is not additive. Lykken, McGue, Tellegen, and Bouchard (1992) describe various traits, such as extroversion, EEG alpha frequency, and facial beauty, that seem to arise through the configuration or interaction of separate, independent traits. These nonadditive, "emergenic" traits are associated with marked MZ similarity and weak DZ similarity—that is, they are genetically mediated but do not tend to run in families. In contrast, the metric traits explored in this *Monograph* all show substantial DZ similarity as well as MZ similarity and thus seem more amenable to a traditional polygenic-additive model.

Estimates of genetic effects in the model used in this study also assume that the genetic resemblance between spouses is negligible. When assortative mating brings together parents of similar genetic makeup, the genetic similarity of their DZ twins is greater than the 50% estimated for random pairings, and genetic effects are underestimated. This is particularly problematic for the assessment of cognitive competencies, for Bouchard and McGue (1981) have noted that spouses tend to be similar on measures of intelligence. For the present cohort, parents' IQs are highly correlated, which suggests a considerable degree of assortative mating. This relation could cause the estimates of genetic similarity presented in this *Monograph* to be conservative, but this criticism is blunted because assortative mating here is on the basis of adult form, whereas the comparisons that are reported are of infant similarities.

The twin analysis model assumes that the environments are essentially the same for both members of an MZ or a DZ twin pair. Three arguments can be adduced in support of this assumption. First, most parents do not know with any certainty whether their same-sex infant twins are MZ or DZ. Differences in the prenatal environment of MZ twins can affect birth weight and produce profound differences in appearance and habits. And DZ twins may be remarkably similar in physical appearance and in other ways that lead parents to infer zygosity. Second, although the MZ-DZ distinction is of concern for researchers, it is of relatively little significance for most parents of twins. The salient issue for these parents is the practical implication of caring for twins: the fact that twins are MZ or DZ probably accounts for little extra variance in their activities.

Finally, if parents know the zygosity of their twins and this information is salient in their provision of an environment, why should we assume that parents provide more similar environments for MZ twins than DZ twins? Benefits of similar treatment (e.g., convenience or cuteness) apply equally to MZ and same-sex DZ twins. Indeed, it seems just as likely that parents in this situation would attempt to promote *differences* between MZ twins rather than similarity (Vandenberg, 1976). A series of reports by Tourrette and Robin (Robin, Josse, Casati, Kherova, & Tourette, 1993; Tourette, Robin, & Josse, 1988, 1989) suggest that mothers of twins may fall into two groups: a difference-promoting group and a difference-diminishing group. Thus, in the unlikely event that parents do exert a special influence on the environments of MZ twins, that influence is as likely to promote difference as similarity.

The equal environments assumption is violated if MZ twin pairs have environments that are more similar, experience their environments more similarly (Lykken, McGue, & Tellegen, 1987; Scarr & McCartney, 1983), or encounter environmental influences that are not shared (Plomin & Daniels, 1987). The latter two possibilities are difficult to test because we do not have introspective reports of what it is like to be an infant twin and because we do not have efficient tools for measuring each twin's unique environment. But our analyses of DZ twin pairs suggest that, if infant twins who look the same are treated the same, this similarity in treatment has no obvious behavioral consequences for the cognitive measures reported here. Matheny, Wilson, and Dolan (1976) used a similar approach for comparing the physical similarity of older twins. They, too, found no relation between similarity of appearance and similarity of performance on a variety of behaviors, including IQ and speech articulation.

Asserting the null hypothesis is problematic both statistically and logically, but the failure to find a relation between the physical similarity and the behavioral similarity of DZ twins bolsters faith in the behavioral genetic model. Interpretation of a relation between physical similarity and behavioral similarity would be difficult, as genetic factors, environmental factors, or both could be responsible. However, the lack of an effect suggests that the moderate level of physical similarity in DZ twins is not a proxy for genetic similarity, at least for the cognitive variables under investigation here. More important, although we cannot conclude that physically similar and dissimilar twins are treated the same, if there are differences in environment that emerge because of the physical similarity of DZ twins, they do not seem to influence the cognitive variables reported in this *Monograph*.

The results indicating that similarity affects recall memory for location at 14 months are reassuring because they argue against the possibility of a Type II error—the analysis technique used in this study can reveal effects of physical similarity when they are present. It could be that physically similar twins are generally treated more similarly, but it is hard to imagine why this effect would be specific to recall memory for locations at 14 months. A more plausible interpretation is that the experimenter tended to treat physically similar twins the same, but, again, it is unclear why this would affect only recall memory for locations in 14-month-olds. Finally, genetic similarity could be offered as an explanation. Physical similarity may not be a proxy for the sort of genetic similarity that is relevant for most of the behaviors assessed here, but the memory for locations test at 14 months involved more gross motor coordination than other procedures, required the ability to inhibit a prepotent response, and tapped various emotional competencies. One or more of these effects may engage a neural or muscular substrate that is affected by the same genes that affect physical similarity.

A few additional assumptions of the twin analysis model should be mentioned. Note that sex differences for average scores on the cognitive variables must affect our interpretation of the effect of environment. Specifically, because we used only same-sex twin pairs, sex differences make DZ twins appear more similar and thus contribute directly to the variance that is partitioned to shared environment. The boost in shared environmental influence caused by same-sex pairing could be calculated with reference to opposite-sex twin pairs but was estimated here by comparing c^2 values for the entire sample (Table 12 above) with the c^2 values for males and females separately (Table 13 above). The average c^2 values for calculations for males or females were only slightly larger (median values between .02 and .03) than calculations for the entire sample. This lack of discrepancy suggests that the effects of same-sex pairing on estimates of environmental influence are negligible.

Finally, the behavioral genetic model used in this study separates the effects of genes and environment, but it is likely that these domains interact. For example, a genetic predisposition toward enhanced expressive ability might not be expressed in the phenotype of a child whose environment ignores or punishes expressive language. The model used in this study does not detect these interactions, but their influence may be discounted for basic cognitive abilities emerging in a normal range of environments. Interactions between genotype and environment are most prominent in extreme circumstances (e.g., when selective breeding is used to enhance genetic effects or when environments are engineered to be outside the normal range).

Effect estimates in the twin model contain various sources of error, but no source of error is particularly egregious. Moreover, the effects of these errors cause overestimation *and* underestimation of effects. The generalizations supported by the twin study method may be limited, but they are probably acceptable for the cognitive variables assessed here and particularly in the context of cross-age comparisons for the same outcome measures. Finally, note that there are few viable alternative methods for exploring the relative contribution of genes and environment to psychological development in humans.

110

XV. THE DEVELOPMENT OF INTELLIGENCE

The primary contribution of this *Monograph* is the identification of genetic and environmental effects on intelligence. However, some of the analyses are relevant for a general description of intellectual development in the second year. We begin the discussion of the development of intelligence with a consideration of four themes—the nature of change, the stability of individual differences, sex differences, and the relation among measures—and then conclude with a general discussion of developmental transitions.

CHANGE IN INTELLECTUAL ABILITY

Development implies change over time, so one important question is how the variables measured here change during the second year. A traditional approach is to look at age-related group differences. The primary focus for age group comparisons in this study was between groups tested at 14, 20, and 24 months, but it is interesting to note that there are also age effects *within* each age bracket. The positive correlations between assessment age and nonverbal, expressive, and receptive constructs for each age bracket underscore the profound effect of age but also indicate an additional source of error variance.[15]

MDI scores are age corrected, so this variable does not reveal change over time for the relatively normal sample tested here. Analyses of group means on the specific constructs suggest a more or less linear increase across the second year, but some pairs of contiguous ages are not significantly different for some measures. To explore differences in the pattern of quantitative change, we classified each child's scores on the nonverbal, expressive, and

---

[15] In the Cholesky decomposition, most error of measurement is partitioned to the effect of unique environment. Because both members of each twin pair were tested at the same time, the error variance of age within age bracket will be attributed to the effect of shared family environment.

receptive measures as indicating early change (i.e., a large increase between 14 and 20 months), late change (i.e., a large increase between 20 and 24 months), or continuous change (i.e., equal increases between 14 and 20 months and between 20 and 24 months). For the nonverbal construct, one-third of infants have patterns that either are indeterminate or indicate no change. This effect also emerges in analyses of the mean linear coefficient and the range, both of which indicate lowest values for the nonverbal measure.

This pattern of results suggests that nonverbal items tend to promote the age constancy that is the hallmark of the MDI. However, when change on the nonverbal measure does occur, it is most likely between 20 and 24 months. This could reflect the age-based placement of items (i.e., the nonverbal items typically administered at 24 months could be relatively easy), but it could also point toward a transition in cognitive ability late in the second year for many infants (i.e., infants do well on the nonverbal items typically administered at 24 months because they have become better able to perform the sorts of skills tapped by these items). For example, many of the items not yet passed uniformly at 20 months involve speed, persistence, and fine motor dexterity.

In contrast, percentage correct for items in the expressive and receptive language composites tends to fall into one of the three categories of change, with most children manifesting either early change or continuous change. Again, this may say more about the age placement of items than about the development of intelligence in children, but the pattern of change is consistent with the well-established fact that the function describing lexical development for most children has a relatively steep slope early in the second year. The data reported here suggest that many twins may exhibit this so-called vocabulary spurt. Early change is more likely for receptive language than expressive language, which would be predicted from studies that show comprehension emerging well before production. Finally, note that a third of the twins have a pattern of continuous change rather than a vocabulary spurt. This phenomenon has been noted previously in more finely grained analyses (e.g., Goldfield & Reznick, 1990; Reznick & Goldfield, 1992) and adds an important constraint on efforts to explain changes in language during the second year: the mechanism that is proposed to explain change in language must account for the fact that some children acquire language without a period of rapid change.

STABILITY AND INSTABILITY OF INDIVIDUAL DIFFERENCES

Previous findings suggest stability of individual MDI scores across the second year, with greater stability for shorter intervals (i.e., a quasi-simplex model). The results reported here suggest stability, but stability between 20 and 24 months is greater than stability between 14 and 20 months for the MDI and each of the three MDI-related constructs. The interpretation of this pattern must be tempered given that the 20–24-month interval is shorter than the 14–20-month interval. However, the 14–20-month correlations, which span a 6-month interval, are no higher than the 14–24-month correlations, which span a 10-month interval. This suggests that it is not the shorter interval between 20 and 24 months that causes increased stability but rather some change in the infant or the measurement late in the second year.

This pattern of increased stability for individual constructs may be related to the increase in the intercorrelation among constructs for older infants, the increase in variability for several measures, and the increase in reliability for most measures. Cronbach's alpha is relatively stable for the nonverbal construct, and Bayley (1969) reports stability across the second year in split-half reliability for the MDI. However, alphas for the expressive and receptive constructs are notably larger at 20 and 24 months, and the estimates of e^2 in the Cholesky decompositions, which indicate error of measurement, among other things, are lower at 20 and 24 months than at the earlier assessment. Considered together, these effects suggest the general statement that the behaviors that we regard as intelligent (e.g., the ability to speak, comprehend, attend, imitate, solve problems) become increasingly amenable to measurement or increasingly stable late in the second year. From the perspective of developmental transitions, these data suggest that change in month-to-month stability is more likely to occur before 20 months.

SEX DIFFERENCES

The main locus for sex effects is age-related group differences: females have higher scores than males on all measures except visual attentiveness, and the differences tend to be largest at 20 and 24 months. Sex differences do not emerge as significant effects in the analysis of quantitative developmental functions, but females tend to have more change between 14 and 20 months, and males tend to have more change between 20 and 24 months. The distribution of change is relative within each group: males change more late in the second year but still lag behind females at 24 months.

The claim that girls are more intelligent than boys during the second year is merely descriptive and does not explain the present phenomenon. Possible mechanisms for the effect include neurological and muscular processes that mature faster in the female, socialization differences in emotional communication (Robinson & Biringen, 1995), and temperamental differences that make females easier to test. Indeed, the standard deviations in Table 5 above suggest that female infants are less variable on most measures, but the differences are small. It is also possible that male-female differences in language are fundamental. The language advantage for infant girls has been questioned (Macaulay, 1978; Reznick, 1990), but recent reports indicate notable gender differences during the second year in production (Hutten-locher et al., 1991) and comprehension (Reznick & Goldfield, 1992). Our results affirm the conclusion that girls have an advantage in language late in the second year.

RELATION AMONG MEASURES

We partitioned the MDI into separable constructs and included some additional measures. As noted earlier, the variables become increasingly inter-correlated for older infants but are well below unity. The analyses reported earlier provided several useful perspectives on the relation among measures.

Expressive versus Receptive Constructs

Focusing first on the language variables, the results indicate strong corre-lations between expressive and receptive language at each age. Note that this relation is not simply a general effect of MDI—the correlations between expressive and receptive language remain robust when the effect of MDI is removed. The similarity between expressive and receptive language is also present in the distribution of quantitative developmental functions. In-fants tend to change earlier on the receptive measure, which is reasonable given the well-established fact that comprehension precedes production, but individual infants tend to show the same pattern of change for both mea-sures.

A relation between the expressive and the receptive lexicon is reasonable because both aspects of language depend on the same sorts of representa-tions and mappings. The findings here are consistent with previous reports but must be integrated with the results reported earlier, and discussed later, that indicate discrepancies between genetic and environmental effects on each language measure and on their correspondence at various ages. As noted earlier, expressive and receptive language measures had a similar distri-bution of quantitative developmental function. However, there is a disparity in cross-classification with the nonverbal measure: the receptive and nonver-bal quantitative developmental functions tend to be similar within individuals, but the expressive and nonverbal quantitative developmental functions are not.

A similar discrepancy emerges in an exploration of the relation between expressive language, receptive language, and the MDI. Expressive and receptive constructs will be related to the MDI because of shared items, but we were able to use expressive and receptive items from the SICD to explore the relation between MDI and constructs that did not share items with the MDI. This analysis indicates that, at each age and across ages, receptive items account for the largest proportion of variance in the MDI. We did not have an independent, broadly based assessment of infant nonverbal ability, which would probably have claimed the lion's share of the variance, but this analysis does indicate the diagnostic significance of receptive language as compared with expressive language.

One parsimonious interpretation of the strong relation between the receptive and the nonverbal measures is that it reflects shared method variance. For example, receptive language skills allow children to understand instructions and, thus, perform better on nonverbal items. From this perspective, it would not be surprising that expressive language is not related to nonverbal ability because nonverbal items, by definition, require no expressive language from the infant. However, while language ability might affect performance on some nonverbal items, we included items in this composite on the basis of the criterion that the item not require the comprehension or use of language. In addition, if comprehension of instructions is relevant for the nonverbal items, it should also be relevant for performance on most expressive language questions in the sense that infants will perform better if they understand that they are being asked to speak.

A second methodological interpretation of the present findings is that the relatively large number of receptive items (in comparison to the number of expressive items) allows receptive language to be assessed more accurately. This enhanced accuracy for the receptive score would bolster correlations with the nonverbal measure, which is also based on a large number of items. However, despite differences in the number of items used to assess expressive and receptive abilities, the continuity of expressive and receptive language over time and the relation between expressive and receptive language and other variables are about the same. Indeed, given these similarities and the relatively public nature of expressive language as opposed to the private nature of receptive language, one could argue that perhaps more receptive items are necessary to obtain the same level of accuracy.

From a theoretical perspective, the strong relations between receptive language and the nonverbal measures are compatible with research by Thal and her colleagues (Thal & Bates, 1988; Thal et al., 1991) indicating that children with delays in expressive language have significant correlations between comprehension and various cognitive measures. It also supports the claim by Bates et al. (1988) and Rescorla (1984) that individual differences in receptive language in the second year may be an early indication of intellectual ability or may play a causal role in subsequent cognitive development (i.e., infants with better receptive abilities acquire more knowledge and skills or do so more easily). In the present circumstance, better receptive language could also account for variance in MDI because infants with better receptive skills may be more likely to pay attention to test materials or cooperate with the examiner. In contrast, performance on expressive items could be related to conversational skill and temperamental factors that affect willingness to talk in a novel or uncertain situation but that do not affect performance on most cognitive tasks.

Qualitative Developmental Function

Qualitative developmental function generally refers to changes in the prominence or salience of abilities that characterize the infant at a particular point in development. A vast battery of measures from assorted domains would be needed to establish an absolute description of qualitative developmental function, but the set of constructs used in this study allows a relative perspective on changes in the prominence of nonverbal, expressive, and receptive abilities during the second year. Previous work by McCall et al. (1977) used a similar frame (i.e., the set of MDI questions) and identified points in development associated with instability of individual differences and a change in the composition of the first principal component that characterizes MDI scores at successive ages. These periods of instability and realignment suggest a series of developmental stages, with stability between 14 and 18 months and between 21 and 27 months and, thus, with a major transition during the second year between 18 and 21 months.

Our results are compatible with the data reported by McCall et al. (1977). Their first principal component for 14–18 months contained mostly language items and fewer nonverbal items, and verbal labeling (expressive or receptive) continued to dominate test behavior at 21, 24, and 27 months. The fact that these contents do not change argues against a major shift in qualitative function (i.e., expressive ability and receptive ability seem to be salient throughout the second year). The findings reported here are compatible with that view. We also found relative dominance for verbal items over nonverbal items across the second year. McCall et al. did not distinguish between expressive and receptive items, but we found relative equity between performance on these two aspects of language. This analysis may be of limited theoretical usefulness because it reflects the distribution of questions on the MDI. But, as will be described later, comparisons of MZ and DZ twins on these measures are more informative.

DEVELOPMENTAL TRANSITIONS IN THE SECOND YEAR

Infants were tested at 14, 20, and 24 months so that we could observe transitions in cognitive development that occur midway to late in the second year. As noted earlier, previous work by McCall et al. (1977) indicates an instability at about 20 months in successive correlations of MDI scores. Other developmentalists have also suggested various transitions during the second year.

Kagan (1981), for example, posits the emergence of a sense of self as the qualitative change that underlies various changes late in the second year (e.g., concern with normative standards, smiling as an accompaniment to mastery, and awareness of feelings, intentions, and competence), and Lewis and Brooks-Gunn (1979) arrive at a similar formulation. Developmental psycholinguists note qualitative change associated with linguistic milestones in the second year, such as the emergence of two-word combinations, the spurt in productive vocabulary, and the dissociation of receptive and expressive language (Anisfeld, 1984; Bates et al., 1988; Bloom, 1970, 1973; Nelson, 1973). Ruff and Rothbart (1996) mention a qualitative change in attentional skills at around 18–24 months. Meltzoff (1990) and Meltzoff and Gopnik (1989) suggest that, beginning at 18 months, infants undergo a profound change in their ability to remember past experiences and to generate hypothetical alternatives. Diamond, Towle, and Boyer (1994) and Overman (1990) report that children show dramatic improvements in their ability on delayed-non-match-to-sample tasks between 18 and 21 months. Finally, the traditional Piagetian view of cognitive development (e.g., Piaget, 1952) posits numerous stage-like changes in ability, several of which would suggest a major transition in development beginning at around 18 months (e.g., infants become able to form mental representations of objects or actions that are not perceptually present, to defer imitation, and to find objects that have undergone an invisible displacement).

The design used in this study provides relatively few assessments per infant and taps a limited range of psychological constructs and thus does not allow a detailed specification of the timing and nature of developmental transitions. However, to the extent that the present data are relevant, the picture that emerges is of a broad array of changes rather than a single general transition at a particular point in time. There are some changes early in the second year, particularly for verbal compared to nonverbal measures and for receptive compared to expressive skills, and the period from 14 to 20 months is associated with relative instability of cross-time correlations. Later in the second year, there is increasing coherence among measures, and there are also stronger relations between infant cognitive ability and such other effects as parents' education. A generous interpretation of these changes might imply an enhanced integration among various facets of cognitive processing, but, as noted earlier, we cannot rule out the possibility that one aspect of this transition is that older infants are simply easier to test or that the measures used in this study are more accurate at later ages.

XVI. GENETIC AND ENVIRONMENTAL
INFLUENCES ON INTELLIGENCE

AGE-SPECIFIC EFFECTS

The correlation between mid-parent education and mid-twin scores for many of the cognitive measures is small at 14 months and appreciably larger at 20 and 24 months. Mother's education is an acceptable proxy for socioeconomic status (Mayes & Bornstein, 1995; Rose et al., 1991), and the correlation at 24 months replicates previous work (e.g., Kopp & Vaughn, 1982). However, the relation between mid-parent education and mid-twin cognitive development is ambiguous because it could reflect effects of heredity, environment, or both. Parents may have more years of education because they have strong cognitive ability (and are thus more likely to thrive in school) or because they are motivated to achieve (and are thus more likely to acquire educational experience). Offspring of educated parents may perform better on cognitive tasks because they inherit a predilection toward cognitive ability or achievement motivation or because educated parents are more likely to provide experiences that stimulate the cognitive development of their offspring (e.g., provide more books and age-appropriate toys, interact more, encourage and reinforce intellectual behaviors). Finally, the increasing relation between parents' education and child performance could be caused by some age-related change in emphasis in the measurement instruments (e.g., the child's increasing use of language, which exposes similarities between the child and the parent) or a general improvement in accuracy. However, as noted earlier, reliability estimates for the MDI and the nonverbal construct remain stable across the second year, but the relation to mid-parent education for these variables changes profoundly.

MDI

Twin correlations for MDI scores increased across the second year, but the difference between MZ and DZ twins remained constant, with higher correlations for MZ than for DZ twins. This pattern of correlations suggests moderate and stable heritability across the second year (with h^2 estimates of .39, .34, and .45 at 14, 20, and 24 months, respectively) and a significant effect of shared environment late in the first year (with c^2 estimates of .45 and .37 at 20 and 24 months).

Longitudinal data on young twins are rare, but there are some points of overlap between our investigation and the data that have been gathered in Louisville. Wilson (1983) reports MDI scores for approximately 100 MZ and DZ twins at 12, 18, and 24 months. Stability values and MZ correlations are similar across the two studies (e.g., Louisville Twin Study MZ correlations are .68, .82, and .81 at 12, 18, and 24 months, respectively, versus the values here of .58, .80, and .83 at 14, 20, and 24 months, respectively). However, the Louisville MZ correlation at 12 months is notably higher that the value reported here. DZ correlations in the Louisville Twin Study are also relatively high, with values of .63, .65, and .73 at 12, 18 and 24 months, respectively, versus the present cohort's values of .38, .64, and .61 at 14, 20, and 24 months, respectively. Indeed, the DZ correlations assessed early in the second year in the two studies are significantly different ($z = 2.71$, $p < .01$).

It is important to understand the discrepancy between Louisville Twin Study correlation values and values reported here, particularly for DZ twin correlations, because these differences cause markedly different estimates of h^2 across the second year. The most likely source of the discrepancy between the two studies is differences in sample characteristics. We instituted recruitment procedures to generate a sample of twins with relatively heavy birth weights, and the families in the present cohort tended to be relatively well educated. In contrast, the Louisville Twin Study used a nonselected sample and thus included many infants who were small for gestational age and who experienced perinatal problems that could have influenced intellectual performance. There are strong correlations in the Louisville Twin Study sample between birth weight and MDI scores in the first and second years (Wilson, 1977; Wilson & Harpring, 1972). Plomin (1986, 1988) has speculated that shared perinatal influences will inflate twin correlations. If one assumes that MZ correlations on the MDI approach a ceiling, then this effect would tend to boost DZ correlations and could produce the pattern of discrepancy observed here. The problem is exacerbated given that assessment is at 12 months in the Louisville study and at 14 months in the present study, for, as our results confirm, younger twins are more vulnerable to the effects of low birth weight.

Another potential difference between the present sample and the Louisville sample is in parents' IQ. Direct comparisons between parents' IQ in the two studies are not available, but it seems likely that the heterogeneous Louisville sample had a broader distribution of parents' IQ and a larger proportion of parents with relatively little education. This increased variability could amplify the effects of assortative mating, which would inflate DZ correlations based on the Louisville Twin Study data. The results reported in this *Monograph* remind us that estimates of effect size for heritable and environmental influences are not general facts of nature but rather apply to the particular sample from which they are derived.

The Louisville Twin Study DZ correlations for the MDI are relatively large and have yielded estimates of h^2 that are relatively small. This is problematic for the interpretation of developmental models derived from the Louisville data (e.g., DeFries, Plomin, & LaBuda, 1987; Eaves, Long, & Heath, 1986). In contrast, our data indicate a pattern of h^2 values at 14, 20, and 24 months that suggests relatively moderate and consistent heritable variation in general mental ability across the second year. Moreover, the MZ and DZ twin correlations observed here at 20 and 24 months (.80 vs. .64 and .83 vs. .61, respectively) are remarkably close to the median twin correlation values of .81 and .61 reported by McCartney et al. (1990) on the basis of a meta-analysis of general intelligence scores from all twin studies published between 1967 and 1985. Note also that heritability estimates reported by Fulker et al. (1988) for MDI scores at 12 and 24 months were relatively low compared with the values here (which may reflect differences in a twin as opposed to an adoption model) but changed little across the second year, which is compatible with the consistent heritability reported here.

The pattern of consistent heritability across the second year suggests a ceiling on heritable influences on individual differences in intelligence that is reached very early in life. This consistency of heritability can be contrasted with the developmental model proposed by Fulker et al. (1988) on the basis of data from the Colorado Adoption Project in which heritability increases between the first and the seventh birthdays. Additional analyses may clarify the methodological and statistical differences that cause this marked discrepancy for estimates of genetic effects on intelligence and reconcile these two divergent views of development. However, one salient source of difference is that the MDI is used only for children up to 2 years of age and that other measures of intelligence are calculated for older children.

Specific Constructs

One valuable aspect of the present study is that we can determine whether age-specific genetic and environmental effects on the MDI are consistent across constructs. Twin correlations for the nonverbal MDI items are notably larger for MZ than DZ twins at each age, producing strong estimates of h^2 (.50 or greater at each age). The same effect emerged for visual attentiveness, with twin correlations almost identical to values for the nonverbal construct. Finally, twin correlations for memory for locations scores were larger for MZ twins at each age, producing significant, although small, effects of h^2 at 14 and 20 months. This pattern is consistent with conclusions derived on the basis of the MDI but suggests an even stronger genetic effect for these nonverbal cognitive abilities.

The consistent results across the three nonverbal measures invite the hypothesis that there is a set of fundamental cognitive processes that are language independent and that unfold during the second year under strong genetic constraints. This construct reflects diverse cognitive abilities, such as the child's ability to gather new information, to retain information, to compare new information with existing knowledge, to understand and apply causal principles, and to imitate the actions of others. Alternatively, or, perhaps, additionally, these nonverbal measures could reflect traits that might be temperamental, such as mastery motivation, persistence, or distractibility. For example, Saudino and Eaton (1995) report genetic effects on activity level in twins younger and older than the twins tested here. It seems likely that an extremely active child would perform relatively poorly on the nonverbal items. Whatever the mechanism, the nonverbal construct seems to be the locus of genetic effects on the MDI and is affected only slightly by shared environment.

Age-specific twin correlations for expressive language are moderate at 14 months and are comparable for MZ and DZ twins. Twin correlations are notably larger at 20 months, with increased differences between MZ and DZ correlations at 20 and 24 months. This pattern suggests a strong effect of shared environment on expressive language across the second year. The difference between MZ and DZ twin correlations also indicates the emergence of a genetic effect on verbal expressiveness late in the second year. Age-specific twin correlations for receptive language are large and relatively similar for MZ and DZ twins, which suggests significant shared environmental effects at each age. The word-comprehension scores provided an additional view of receptive language ability. Twin correlations were much lower than the values for the receptive construct, but the pattern was the same. That is, twin correlations on word comprehension were comparable for MZ and DZ twins, replicating the effect of shared environment at 20 and 24 months. From this perspective, the effects of shared environment on the MDI are clearly effects on language.

Children learn to speak the language that they hear, so environmental effects on language development are not surprising. Language effects could be influenced by factors in the shared environment, such as the quality and quantity of the language the child hears. For example, Huttenlocher et al. (1991) report that individual differences in infant expressive vocabulary are related to the amount that mothers speak to their infants and that the age of acquisition for individual words can be predicted by the frequency of those words in mothers' speech. Other possible environmental influences include differences in parenting style, such as preferred mode of interaction (e.g., tendency to ask questions, responsiveness vs. intrusiveness) or choice of activities (e.g., naming games, book reading). Our data do not allow specification of the environmental mechanisms that affect language, but subsequent work on this topic may be warranted because of the potential usefulness of early interventions that promote language competence.

The genetic effect on expressive language is more intriguing, whatever its exact timing. MZ and DZ twin pairs differ at 20 and 24 months only, but expressive language is rare at 14 months and increases dramatically later in the second year. Thus, the lack of a genetic effect at 14 months could reflect the difficulty of measuring expressive language when the vocabulary is small. This complaint is blunted given that twin correlations at 14 months are moderate and that cross-time correlations for the expressive language measure are comparable to the values reported for other measures, which would not be the case if measurement at 14 months were inadequate. The results reported here suggest that, across the second year, genetic factors play an increasingly significant role in the child's expressive language.

Locke (Locke, 1990; Locke & Mather, 1989) has argued for the innateness of phonological development, and previous research with adoptees indicates that communicative performance in the first year defined across such measures as vocalization, gesture, imitation, and phonological ability is more highly correlated with the birth mother than with the adoptive mother (Hardy-Brown & Plomin, 1985; Hardy-Brown et al., 1981). Communicative competence measures at 2 and 3 years also show genetic as well as environmental effects (Thompson & Plomin, 1988). This study bridges the gap between these reports and suggests that there is genetic influence on expressive language during the second year as well.

The index of expressive language used in this study reflects both the range of the child's expressive vocabulary and the child's willingness to communicate in the presence of an unfamiliar examiner. Genetics could affect the size of the expressive lexicon. For example, Huttenlocher et al. (1991) suggest that there are genetic influences on the child's capacity to learn from input. However, this interpretation would also suggest genetic effects on receptive language, but these effects are weak at 20 and 24 months. Thus, we favor an interpretation in which the genetic effect on expressive language is mediated by temperamental factors. This aspect is particularly salient in the present context because an unwillingness to talk in an unfamiliar situation is related to a heritable temperamental disposition toward shyness and fearfulness (Robinson et al., 1992) and is more likely among MZ twins (DiLalla et al., 1994). The measure of expressive language used in this study is related to knowledge (e.g., the expressive measure is correlated with the receptive measure), but a considerable amount of variance may be accounted for by other influences, such as discourse ability and talkativeness. Further research with twins should assess the competence component of expressive ability, which can be measured using extensive recordings of spontaneous production (e.g., as in Huttenlocher et al., 1991). This aspect of expressive ability can be contrasted with the performance component tapped by the measurement procedures used in this study.

The presence of a same-aged sibling certainly alters the linguistic environment. However, if one assumes that twin language is essentially normal in most respects, our data highlight the need to disentangle genetic and environmental influences on language development. For example, the data reported here are compatible with the hypothesis that expressive parents will have expressive children. Without a genetic analysis, it would be tempting to conclude that the environment's role is causal through the mechanism of expressive parents providing their children with a rich linguistic environment or, perhaps, expressive children evoking a rich linguistic environment from adults.

Hampson and Nelson (1993), for example, find differences between the mothers of children who are early and late talkers and note two directions of effect—differences among mothers could enable some children to talk earlier, or mothers might differ as a result of responding differentially to their child's language ability. Hoff-Ginsberg (1991, 1994) has demonstrated that differences in how much mothers talk to their children generally reflect differences in their tendencies toward talkativeness (e.g., talkative mothers talk more to an examiner) and their discourse style (e.g., talkative mothers produce multiple utterances on a single topic). Our results extend Hoff-Ginsberg's suggestion into a different causal domain: genetic mechanisms that affect individual differences in adult speech and that are transmitted to offspring may also promote individual differences in the child's expressive language and, hence, early or late talking. Additional work is needed to explore these possibilities, but, as Hardy-Brown and Plomin (1985) have suggested, twin analysis allows a correction to correlational studies that confound environmental influence with genetic influence.

Sex Differences

Sex differences between MZ and DZ twin correlations can be calculated, but the reduced sample size creates DeFries-Fulker models that reveal only the most robust effects and interactions. Indeed, the parameters for interactions with sex are significant for visual attention only. This lack of statistically significant sex-related interactions could discourage speculation about male-female differences, but large samples of infant twins are rare, and it seems wasteful not to take a tentative look at the sex-specific twin correlations and the estimated age-specific effects (Schmidt, 1996).

The most obvious pattern in the MZ and DZ correlations for males and females is that MZ correlations tend to be greater for males than females and that DZ correlations tend to be greater for females than males. Thus, strong genetic effects for males emerge for the nonverbal, expressive, and receptive constructs at most ages. In contrast, correlations for females suggest a stronger effect of the environment, particularly on the measures of language later in the second year. The only anomalous variable is visual attention, for which separate correlations for males and females suggest that males are somewhat affected by shared environment, but this pattern changes over age. Females show a consistent genetic effect. This task-specific sex difference may emerge because of the linguistic context of the visual attentiveness measure. As noted earlier, phenotypic differences on this measure may have a different meaning for infants as a function of their interest in the naming game.

These findings raise the speculative but intriguing suggestion that genetic and environmental effects for some aspects of cognitive ability may have different effects on individual differences for males and females. The assertion of strong genetic effects for males is not new: there was considerable debate during the 1960s and 1970s concerning the possibility that spatial ability is influenced by a major gene on the X chromosome (for a critical summary, see Plomin 1986). A recessive allele on the X chromosome is less likely to be expressed in females because it must be present on both X chromosomes. Thus, if an ability is affected by a gene on the X chromosome, this effect could be more likely for males. It is extremely unlikely that one X-based allele accounts for the broad range of variables on which males show stronger genetic effects, but note that the difference occurs primarily for the nonverbal and language constructs. Some general aspect of temperament that is X linked and that affects performance on the MDI could account for the range of findings.

Our results also suggest that shared environmental effects are greater for females. This relation between heredity and environment could be merely complementary (i.e., strong genetic effects decrease the variance available for environmental effects, and strong environmental effects decrease the variance available for genetic effects). It is also possible that the effects emerge because females are more attuned to the environment. For example, given that females have better verbal abilities, their language skills provide a greater opportunity for them to engage and mediate the environment and thus allow the environment to influence individual differences. This interpretation also explains the developmental differences in effects: individual differences in expressive language become increasingly heritable for males and increasingly affected by shared environment for females. Comparable effects would also emerge if females spend more time in cooperative play or in proximity to parents, thus creating more opportunities for the environment to affect them. The limited power to resolve genetic and environmental effects when our sample is segregated by sex precludes firm support for any particular finding, but the consistency across measures suggesting stronger genetic effects on males and stronger environmental effects on females deserves further study.

Relations among Measures

Our data allow us to go beyond a description of qualitative developmental function and explore genetic and environmental influences. We find that performance on nonverbal items relative to verbal items is more similar for MZ twin pairs than for DZ twin pairs, particularly at 20 months. This suggests a genetic influence on qualitative developmental function throughout the second year and particularly during the psychological transition that is posited to occur late in the second year. The pattern of effects for expressive and receptive measures is notably different in that DZ twins are quite similar at 20 and 24 months, which suggests an environmental influence on the tendency to excel at expressive as opposed to receptive language. The absence of a relation between expressive and receptive language at 24 months for MZ twins as compared with DZ twins could occur for various reasons but is anomalous and requires replication before an interpretation is warranted.

A more complex view of genetic and environmental effects on the relation among measures emerges in the age-specific Cholesky decompositions, which indicate the overlap and distinctiveness of genetic and environmental influences on the nonverbal, expressive, and receptive constructs. There are distinct genetic influences on the nonverbal and receptive measures at 14 months. There is also a minor path that overlaps the two measures, but the most salient effect is separate influences. This suggests that the significant effects of h^2 on nonverbal and receptive constructs at 14 months and on the balance between verbal and nonverbal measures are mediated by separate genetic influences. This pattern of separate influences continues at 20 months, with one genetic influence on the nonverbal construct and one genetic effect that overlaps the two language constructs (although the h^2 values at 20 months are not significant). At 24 months, there is a shared genetic effect across all three measures, but it is strongest for the nonverbal construct. Thus, although there is some overlap between genetic influence on nonverbal and genetic influence on verbal domains, there is sufficient differentiation at 20 months to support the hypothesis of genetic influence on the transition in qualitative developmental function.

For shared environment, the Cholesky decomposition indicates strong overlapping influences on the significant effects of expressive and receptive language at 14 months. A minor path overlaps with the nonsignificant nonverbal construct, but the strong overlap is between expressive and receptive language. At 20 and 24 months, one effect of shared environment overlaps all

125

three domains. There is little effect of shared environment on the nonverbal construct. It is interesting to note that a second shared environmental influence affects both language measures at 20 months. However, this influence makes twins similar on one aspect of language and different on the other. The specific locations of the different signs are arbitrary but indicate that the same influence promotes similarity on one measure and difference on the other. For example, parents who focus on training infants to know the names of objects and people might induce similarity on receptive language; this same strategy could amplify differences in expressive language. At 24 months, an environmental influence affects expressive language and not receptive language. These two findings, which indicate different effects of shared environment on expressive and receptive language, are compatible with the DeFries-Fulker analysis of the difference between expressive and receptive language: environmental effects late in the second year can promote differences between expressive and receptive language scores.

CONTINUITY AND CHANGE OVER TIME IN GENETIC AND SHARED ENVIRONMENTAL INFLUENCES

Change in the efficacy of genetic and environmental effects at different ages is a salient facet of development. Recent advances in theory and methodology have provided access to an additional facet: the genetic and environmental influences that promote longitudinal continuity and change. A particular genetic or environmental effect might exert its influence diachronically and thus account for the same phenotypic variance across ages. Alternatively, a genetic or environmental effect might account for unique variance at successive ages and thus promote change. As a preliminary approach to this question, consider the analysis of quantitative developmental functions. Wilson (1983) looked at patterns of spurts and lags in cognitive development in the Louisville sample and found greater synchrony among MZ twins. Genetic effects on spurts and lags suggest that continuity and change in cognitive development derive in part from heritable influences. Note that this analysis does not separate the influence of continuity and change but rather subsumes both as manifestations of a genetic mechanism that influences the pattern of development. We can apply a comparable logic to our analyses of quantitative developmental function. Specific patterns of quantitative developmental function can be identified, and these patterns are a gross reflection of influences on continuity and change. The question of interest is the relative similarity of quantitative developmental function for MZ and DZ twin pairs.

For the nonverbal construct, the contingency coefficients that measure twin pair similarity on quantitative developmental function are somewhat larger for MZ twins. Comparable analyses of the linear coefficient and range (other aspects of quantitative developmental function) also indicate strong heritability. This suggests a genetic influence on continuity and change, but the effect is fragile because relatively few infants show systematic patterns of change on this measure. For expressive language, the contingency coefficients (or correlations) for all three measures of quantitative developmental function are significant for both MZ and DZ twins, and the DeFries-Fulker analysis indicates some genetic and environmental influence. Finally, for receptive language, indices of quantitative developmental function are large but are more nearly comparable for MZ and DZ twins, which suggests effects of shared environment. These findings indicate that the genetic effects on spurts and lags reported by Wilson (1983) might be decomposed into a set of genetic and environmental influences on continuity and change in different measures. However, the analysis of quantitative developmental function does not reveal the specific pattern.

A more powerful approach for detecting continuity and change in genetic and environmental influences is to construct models in which cross-twin, cross-time correlations are used to estimate influences that are associated with the same phenotypic variance across time and influences that emerge afresh at each assessment.

Genetic Effects

Previous analyses of MDI scores by Cardon et al. (1992), Cherny, Fulker, Emde, et al. (1994), and Plomin et al. (1993) indicate substantial genetic continuity of general cognitive ability between 14 and 24 months but significant new genetic variance at 24 months. The componential view adopted here indicates that this statement is reasonably accurate for the nonverbal construct: there is a genetic effect on continuity in the nonverbal construct, but there are also genetic effects associated with change at each age. In contrast, the genetic effect on language promotes only continuity, with that continuity from 20 months for expressive language and from 14 months for receptive language.

Genetic continuity and change seem to imply the activity of structural genes, but genetic influences can be interpreted more broadly to encompass any mechanisms associated with trait-relevant genetic variability. Genetic continuity in the nonverbal, expressive, and receptive constructs could imply the influence of some fundamental and heritable aspect of the nervous system (e.g., the number of dendritic spines, the level of specific neurotransmitters) or a genetic influence on some trait that affects performance on these three constructs (e.g., attentiveness, fearfulness, cooperativeness, visual acuity). Genetic change for the nonverbal construct suggests that one or more physiolog-

127

ical or psychological processes change at 20 and at 24 months and, thus, that genetic mediation is likely to play a role in transition late in the second year.

Shared Environment

Cardon et al. (1992), Cherny, Fulker, Emde, et al. (1994), and Fulker et al. (1993) report that shared environment promotes continuity in MDI scores, but we find notably different patterns for individual constructs. Shared environment has no effect on the nonverbal composite but pervasive effects on both measures of language, promoting not only continuity across ages but also change at each age. From this perspective, the effects that have been identified for the MDI may offer an unrealistic portrait of shared environment influences on cognitive development. Shared environment has a potent influence on language. Shared environmental effects on continuity could emerge because of such stable aspects of the environment as the parents' interactive styles, strategies for teaching language, and provision of books. Shared environmental influence could also promote change: as infants go from rudimentary use of speech to extensive comprehension and increasingly sophisticated expression, parents have new opportunities to influence language through response to the child's verbalizations, sensitivity to the child's changing capacity for joint visual attention (Morissette, Ricard, & Decarie, 1995), or the provision of language-relevant activities and materials. Alternatively, older twins might become more likely to engage language-relevant aspects of the environment, such as books, siblings, or parents. Cherny, Fulker, Emde, et al. (1994) interpreted the effect of shared environment on continuity of MDI as indicating the efficacy of such stable environmental influences as socioeconomic status. This statement is incomplete because it excludes the shared environmental influences that promote change in language.

It is notable that there is no shared environmental influence on continuity or change for the nonverbal measure. This finding is somewhat surprising in that we often assume that stable environmental influences such as socioeconomic status will affect the child's cognitive abilities. The present sample was relatively homogeneous, which precluded an opportunity to observe environmental effects that emerge on the basis of extreme differences in socioeconomic status. But, given this constraint, family environmental variation had virtually no effect on continuity or change in nonverbal ability. This reinforces the position, stated earlier, that there is a set of genetically determined core cognitive processes that affect phenotypic differences in cognitive ability during the second year. This finding may have implications for interventions applied to infants in the second year. Genetically driven traits can often be modified by intervention (i.e., genetic influence on a trait does not preclude environmental influence), but interventions targeted toward language skills in the second year may be more efficacious than interventions targeted toward nonverbal skills.

THE INFLUENCE OF UNIQUE ENVIRONMENT

The data suggest robust effects of unique or nonshared environment on change across time for each measure (i.e., e^2 is associated with new phenotypic variance at each age). These effects must be interpreted in the context of comparable results reported earlier: moderate to robust influences of unique environment on each measure at each age and robust effects of unique environment on uniqueness among measures at each age, with some slight effect on overlap. These results are compatible with previous reports based on subjects in the present cohort, in the Twin-Infant Project, and in the Colorado Adoption Project that reveal age-specific effects of unique environment and no developmental continuity (Cardon et al., 1992; Fulker et al., 1993). An optimistic reading of these effects would suggest that unique environment has a significant effect on aspects of phenotypic similarity and difference between twins, and there is support for this hypothesis (Dunn & Plomin, 1990; Plomin & Daniels, 1987). However, closer inspection of the results for e^2 suggests some reasons for caution in interpreting these effects.

The fundamental difficulty with our estimate of e^2 is that we did not measure each twin's unique environment but rather estimated e^2 as the residual after h^2 and c^2 were calculated. The disadvantage of this accounting by residual rather than by direct measurement is that intrinsic effects such as error of measurement and random (chaotic) epigenetic processes may strongly influence each twin's score, making it unique. Our confidence in e^2 as an index of extrinsic aspects of the unique environment is eroded by the following facts: First, in the age-specific estimates of effects, e^2 was particularly large for measurements that we would assume contained more error (e.g., the 14-month assessments of the infant's minimal expressive and receptive language, the word-comprehension score at each age as compared with the score for receptive language, and the problematic memory for locations test at each age). Second, the cross-measure and cross-age Cholesky decompositions revealed strong measure-specific and age-specific effects of e^2 but little cross-measure or cross-age continuity.

Cardon et al. (1992) note that some short-term aspects of the unique environment (e.g., illness, fluctuations in mood and state) should have age-specific effects, but it seems reasonable to expect these same aspects to promote strong continuity across measures in the Cholesky decomposition. At each age, there is some evidence for these effects (i.e., unique environmental influences that span measures), but the paths are weak compared with unique environmental influences that are specific to each measure. Furthermore, it

129

also seems reasonable to expect that other equally profound nonshared environmental influences—such as parents' preference for one twin over the other (Lytton, Conway, & Sauve, 1977; Minde, Carter, Goldberg, & Jeffers, 1990), intrauterine nutritional advantages or deficits, birth trauma, long-term illness, or unique aspects of the social or physical environment—should cause some continuity over time for some measures. But, as noted earlier, the cross-age Cholesky models reveal no effects of unique environment indicating continuity across age.

Given that effects of unique environment are relevant for understanding why siblings in a family are different, one possible cause for the lack of continuity observed here is that unique environment has a different meaning for twins than it does for different-aged siblings. Some stable environmental influences tend to stay constant or change very slowly (e.g., parents' education, economic status, temperament, religious and philosophical orientation) and can be contrasted with unstable environmental influences that may change more rapidly (e.g., the time and resources available to parents for child rearing; family configuration; seasonal variation; major household acquisitions, such as a videocassette recorder, a swimming pool, or a playroom). Depending on the rate at which these influences change, unstable environmental influences, which may have a stronger effect on children at one point in development and a weaker effect at another, will be experienced as unique environmental influences for different-aged siblings but as shared environmental influences for twins. Thus, the aspects of the environment that promote dissimilarity in the phenotypes of nontwin siblings can promote similarity in the phenotypes of twins.

A second factor that precludes unique environmental influence on continuity is that current methods of estimating unique environment also capture the random outcomes that emerge when chaotic epigenetic processes create variability under constant genetic and environmental conditions (Kurnit, Layton, & Matthysse, 1987; Molenaar, Boomsma, & Dolan, 1993). These self-organizing developmental processes are potent explanations of infant motor development (Goldfield, 1995; Thelen & Smith, 1994) and have been applied to a broad range of psychological phenomena (Smith & Thelen, 1993). To the extent that these processes affect infants in their second year, they will boost the estimate of unique environment but cause a lack of continuity in its effect.

Finally, as Goldsmith (1993) notes, environment as estimated in a behavioral genetic model is not necessarily overt experiences per se but rather the effect of those experiences, whether they create similarity or dissimilarity among twins. A shared experience (e.g., being read to) might engage a more linguistic twin, promoting language development, but frustrate a less linguistic twin, undermining language development. The net effect of this shared experience would be to decrease phenotypic similarity and boost estimates of unique environment. From the present perspective, a more problematic scenario is that parents who expect twins to have comparable abilities might expend more effort on enhancing the linguistic or nonverbal skills of the more slowly developing twin. The effect of this unique environment would be to promote phenotypic similarity and thus boost effects attributed to the shared environment. Note that parents' compensation for twin differences would be particularly problematic for behavioral genetic models if the level of compensation varied for MZ and DZ twins. But, as noted earlier, there are several reasons to doubt that parents treat twins differently in a systematic way as a function of zygosity.

TRANSITIONS IN THE SECOND YEAR

Finally, we can ask about genetic and environmental influences on developmental transitions. Genetic change for the nonverbal construct late in the second year is not surprising given the likelihood that there is some sort of cognitive change for normal infants at about this time. However, as noted earlier, language ability is also a critical component of the transition late in the second year. The analysis of continuity and change reveals an intricate pattern of genetic and environmental effects on language, and age-specific analyses suggest an emergence of genetic effects on expressive language and of shared environmental effects on receptive language. The analysis of qualitative developmental function indicates genetic effects at 20 months on nonverbal versus verbal performance but environmental effects on expressive versus receptive performance. Thus, we are led to the seemingly banal generalization that genetic *and* environmental influences are relevant for an explanation of developmental transitions.

The timing of the genetic effects could emerge because of changes in the biological substrates that support cognitive and lexical ability. For example, the later half of the second year is associated with a rapid acceleration in the number of synapses within and across regions of the cortex (Huttenlocher, 1990) and other neurobiological changes.[16] Changes in language ability during the second year engage a wide range of environmental influences that were less salient for younger infants. For example, infants begin to ask questions (e.g., "What's that?"), emit linguistic behaviors that evoke corrections (e.g., "No—that's not a dog, that's a cat"), and become able to engage in complex dialogue. A similar argument was offered earlier to explain the locus of environmental effects on females. In the present context, these lin-

---

[16] For descriptions of various neurobiological aspects of development, see Bates et al. (1992), Colombo (1995), Dawson and Fischer (1994), Gibson and Petersen (1991), and Quartz and Sejnowski (in press).

guistic abilities, which usually emerge in the second year, establish ample opportunity for environmental effects on a developmental transition.

Transition in the second year is not simply the maturation of some underlying physiological process, or change in temperament, or some other change that can be attributed to the expression of genetically coded products. An adequate explanation of the various transitions must also include effects of environment, such as how parents perceive the child, the nature of the parent-child interaction, or other aspects of the environment. Developmental change in environmental influences seems particularly likely in the linguistic domain. During the second year, language becomes an increasingly salient aspect of the infant's life and engages the environment in increasingly complex ways as parents become conversational partners and informants. Finally, note that genetic and environmental influence could interact. That is, the effects of the environment could become salient at 20 months *because* of some genetically influenced change (e.g., a completed neurological circuit promotes a burst in the lexicon, the infant's communicative ability, or the infant's desire to speak). In this case, a genetically influenced change causes the child to engage the environment in new or newly potent ways.

XVII. CONCLUSION

Our goal in this *Monograph* was to explore the development of intelligence during the second year using the powerful methodology of a multivariate, multimethod, longitudinal twin study. The discussion above highlights the findings that emerge when data from twins are used to explore issues of genetic and environmental influence on age-specific development and on continuity and change from the perspective of individual differences and developmental functions. Behavioral genetic models have limitations but are particularly useful for comparisons among variables measured in a longitudinal design. The parameter estimates reported here are descriptions of a cohort of healthy, middle-class, English-speaking twins with normal birth weights, but they suggest several useful generalizations about cognitive development.

The study of nature reveals many phenomena the description of which can change as a function of the level of magnification: a ball can be described as a solid object or as a configuration of particles moving through a vast, empty space; the mind can be described as a cohesive, self-conscious entity or as an assembly of cells engaged in chemical and electrical interactions. The results reported here extend this hierarchtypic specificity to several aspects of cognitive development.

A contrast can be drawn between the patterns of heritable and environmental influences that are revealed for general and specific measures of cognitive development. The MDI can be construed as a general measure of cognitive ability, akin to the construct *intelligence* when applied to the cognitive domain. The analysis of MDI scores reveals stable genetic effects across the second year with effects of shared environment emerging later. The estimates of heritability for the MDI are comparable to heritability values for intelligence reported for adults, which suggests that a ceiling on heritable influence on intelligence is reached relatively early in life. However, analyses of specific measures of cognitive ability indicate that it is primarily measures of nonverbal ability that support strong effects of heritability, with these analyses indicating age-specific genetic effects and genetic influences on continuity and

133

change. This finding suggests a core set of cognitive processes that unfold during the second year under strong genetic constraints. These cognitive processes, which tap such abilities as solving problems, imitating, and performing fine motor tasks, seem to be relatively independent of linguistic ability, but there is some overlap. Furthermore, in contrast to the results for the MDI, the analysis of nonverbal ability does not reveal evidence of significant effects of shared environment.

This leads to a second contrast: the relation between the measures of expressive and receptive language. Expressive and receptive scores are related (e.g., scores are correlated at each age, and the distributions of quantitative developmental functions are similar), which is reasonable given that both are reflections of the infant's knowledge and require commerce with our lexical code. But the correlation between expressive and receptive scores reflects only 26%–37% of the variance, and there are also differences between the measures (e.g., earlier change for the receptive measure, different relations to other measures). Differences between expressive ability and receptive ability are particularly salient in the behavioral genetic analyses. Age-specific analyses indicate genetic effects on expressive scores late in the second year and environmental effects throughout. Receptive language has some genetic influence at 14 months, but the more salient effect is shared environment, accounting for significant variance in age-specific analyses at 20 and 24 months and in analyses of continuity and change. From the perspective of general effects on the MDI, the environmental effects on MDI late in the second year are clearly effects on language rather than on nonverbal ability.

One reason for the lack of correspondence between expressive and receptive language is that performance on the two measures may reflect the differential operation of additional extralexical processes. The expressive measure, which requires infants to produce language in an unfamiliar context, may be affected by temperamental dispositions (e.g., behavioral inhibition). The receptive measure can have extralexical influences (e.g., motivation), but it seems more likely to reflect lexical knowledge per se and thus the ability to learn from experience. This explains the strong relation between receptive language and the nonverbal measure and between receptive language and the MDI score.

Finally, we find a difference among results for the entire sample, among results calculated separately for males and females, and among results that refer to patterns of individual difference. Mean differences in age emerge across assessments at 14, 20, and 24 months and also for finely grained differences in testing date within each age bracket. However, when the focus is the development of individual infants, we find various patterns of change. These patterns of change sometimes coalesce to suggest general effects (e.g., a rapid burst in the lexicon in the middle of the second year, a correspondence between expressive and receptive measures), but some individuals follow unique paths (e.g., continuous change or no change in the lexicon), and there are some notable differences in development across different measures (e.g., the receptive lexicon increases earlier than the expressive lexicon).

Sex differences emerge in analyses of phenotypic development and estimates of genetic and environmental influences. Infant females attain higher scores on cognitive measures, particularly at 20 and 24 months. This effect may emerge on the basis of maturation or temperamental differences, but language ability is likely to be a significant influence. Genetic effects tend to be stronger in males; environmental effects tend to be stronger in females. This, too, could reflect language differences, as the more verbal females engage the environment in more significant ways than their male counterparts. Caution is necessary in interpreting these patterns because analyses of sex effects are calculated on the basis of a greatly reduced sample size, but the pattern of effects across measures is consistent.

As expected, the multilevel analysis provides a complex array of findings, with some inconsistencies across measures and across subgroups. This statement should not undermine the value of this *Monograph*, but it does suggest guidelines for future research. First, although our sample of over 400 pairs of twins seems large, the unavoidable loss of data and the need to partition this group into various subgroups require that future studies include an even larger sample. Second, we were able to draw reasonable conclusions about genetic and environmental influences using MZ and same-sex DZ twins, but increasingly sophisticated behavioral genetic models will require data from siblings, different-sex twins, and parents. Third, environmental effects would be more convincing if they could be measured directly rather than inferred as a residual, particularly aspects of the linguistic environment. Fourth, we were able to bracket developmental transitions that occur late in the second year, but our longitudinal analyses were still relatively coarse. Development in the second year proceeds rapidly and would be better studied in a design using more frequent assessments. Finally, one of the most useful aspects of this *Monograph* was the comparison of various components of intelligence. Future work should expand this approach and include more measures of specific aspects of nonverbal and verbal ability.

TABLE A1

SICD and BSID Items in the Language and Nonverbal Composites

	Percentage Correct		
	14 Months	20 Months	24 Months
Expressive language			
SICD Expressive Scale:			
22a Name picture of baby	5	54	82
22b Name picture of shoe	3	54	82
22c Name picture of ball	4	54	81
29a Answer question "No"....................	N.A.	N.A.	22
29b Answer question "Yes"	N.A.	N.A.	45
31a Answer question "Shoes"	N.A.	N.A.	24
BSID:			
79 Vocalize 4 syllables	98	100	100
85 Say "Da-Da" or equivalent	95	100	100
101 Jabber expressively	80	97	98
113 Say 2 words	26	90	98
116 Use gestures to make wants known	82	99	100
124 Name 1 object...........................	8	67	90
127 Use words to make wants known	5	69	91
130 Name 1 picture..........................	6	63	89
136 Say sentence of 2 words..................	2	35	74
138 Name 2 objects..........................	0	29	70
141 Name 3 pictures..........................	0	29	72
146 Name 3 objects..........................	0	15	53
149 Name 5 pictures	0	12	52
Receptive language			
SICD Receptive Scale:			
6b Respond to "Come here".................	89	96	98
9 Respond to "Don't touch!"	54	71	86
10 Respond to gesture and "Give it to me"	85	97	99
11a Indicate referents *cup, spoon, shoe*	48	92	98
12a Respond to "Get the car"..................	68	91	98
12b Respond to "Give it to me"	26	60	83
12c Respond to "Put it on the paper"	23	69	89
13a Indicate referent *ears*....................	5	54	79

	PERCENTAGE CORRECT		
	14 Months	20 Months	24 Months
13b Indicate referent *eyes*.....................	17	76	93
13c Indicate referent *hair*	7	69	92
13d Indicate referent *mouth*...................	9	70	93
13e Indicate referent *nose*	16	76	92
14a Respond to "Sit down"	49	87	95
15a Indicate referent *socks*...................	10	69	90
15b Indicate referent *tree*.....................	6	61	87
15c Indicate referent *bear*	11	76	92
15d Indicate referent *chair*...................	5	66	89
15e Indicate referent *key*	7	64	90
15f Indicate referent *box*.....................	5	55	84
16 Respond to "Where's mama?"	55	90	97
17a Respond to "Put block on box"............	1	13	32
17b Respond to "Put block in box"	2	57	79
17c Respond to "Put block beside box"........	0	1	4
17d Respond to "Put block under box"........	0	7	35
18 Respond to "Bye-bye"	25	52	73
19a Respond to "Put 1 spoon in box"	N.A.	6	12
20a Respond to "Let me see you walk"	N.A.	52	82
21a Indicate referent *what mom cooks on*	N.A.	N.A.	36
21b Indicate referent *what you wear on feet*	N.A.	N.A.	42
21c Indicate referent *what you read*	N.A.	N.A.	21
23 Indicate referent *big, little*.................	N.A.	N.A.	25
BSID:			
89 Respond to verbal request.................	97	100	100
94 Respond to "No no!"...................	89	99	100
117 Indicate referent for article of clothing......	25	83	95
126 Respond to command re: doll..............	17	83	96
128 Indicate referents for body parts on doll.....	6	76	95
131 Find 2 hidden objects identified by name....	20	58	71
144 Indicate referent for 2 objects.............	1	43	78
152 Indicate referent for 3 objects.............	0	24	60
158 Respond to 2 prepositions.................	0	15	46
162 Respond to "Put 1 block on the paper".....	0	3	8
163 Respond to 3 prepositions.................	0	3	20
Nonverbal			
BSID:			
74 Attend to scribbling.......................	98	100	100
75 Look for fallen spoon.....................	98	100	100
76 Playful response to mirror	98	100	100
77 Retain 2 of 3 cubes.......................	98	100	100
78 Manipulate ball: notice detail	98	100	100
80 Pull string adaptively: secure ring...........	98	100	100
81 Cooperate in games	97	100	100
82 Attempt to secure 3 cubes	97	100	100
83 Ring bell purposively......................	97	100	100
86 Uncover toy	98	100	100
87 Finger holes in pegboard...................	95	100	100
88 Pick up cup: secure cube..................	98	100	100
90 Put cube in cup on command..............	98	100	100
91 Look for contents of box..................	99	100	100

	PERCENTAGE CORRECT		
	14 Months	20 Months	24 Months
92 Stir with spoon in imitation................	98	99	100
93 Look at pictures in book	99	100	100
95 Attempt to imitate scribbles...............	92	99	100
96 Unwrap cube	85	99	100
97 Repeat performance laughed at	81	98	100
98 Hold crayon adaptively....................	96	99	100
99 Push car along..........................	96	99	100
100 Put 3 or more cubes in cup...............	84	99	100
102 Uncover box............................	88	99	100
103 Turn pages of book......................	94	97	100
104 Imitate patting of doll...................	84	96	98
105 Dangle ring by string	55	92	98
107 Put beads in box	89	99	100
108 Place peg repeatedly.....................	70	100	100
109 Remove pellet from bottle................	85	98	99
110 Place round block on board	60	97	100
111 Build tower of 2 cubes	52	95	99
112 Spontaneous scribble	58	90	98
114 Put 9 cubes in cup	55	93	97
115 Close round box	50	91	97
118 Place pegs in 70 seconds	11	96	99
119 Build tower of 3 cubes	10	78	95
120 Place round block on board	33	81	96
121 Place 2 round blocks on board............	21	88	97
122 Attain toy with stick....................	44	90	97
123 Place peg in 42 seconds..................	5	90	98
125 Imitate crayon stroke	24	83	92
129 Place 2 round and 2 square blocks.........	5	74	93
133 Mend broken doll marginally	5	44	79
134 Place pegs in 30 seconds	1	68	94
135 Differentiate scribble from stroke..........	7	62	83
137 Place all objects on board	2	54	85
140 Mend broken doll approximately	1	27	68
142 Place 6 blocks on board..................	1	53	85
143 Build tower of 6 cubes	0	22	47
147 Imitate vertical and horizontal strokes.......	1	15	40
151 Imitate placement of items on board........	0	25	63
153 Mend broken doll exactly	0	6	34
154 Make train of cubes.....................	0	20	53
155 Place items on board in 150 seconds........	0	28	69
156 Place pegs in 22 seconds	0	30	71
157 Fold paper	0	12	32
159 Place items on board in 90 seconds.........	0	24	65
160 Place items on board in 60 seconds.........	0	14	55.
161 Build tower of 8 cubes	0	5	18

NOTE.—N.A. = not administered at that age.

TECHNIQUE FOR CATEGORIZING PATTERNS OF CHANGE

A Pearson correlation was calculated between each child's three scores (on each measure) and a set of contrast weights that represented each pattern (i.e., for early change, the pattern was 1, 3, 3; for continuous change, the pattern was 1, 2, 3; and, for late change, the pattern was 1, 1, 3). The child was initially categorized into the pattern of change associated with the contrast weight configuration that yielded the highest correlation. For example, a child with nonverbal scores of .63 at 14 months, .84 at 20 months, and .88 at 24 months had correlations of .99 with the early change pattern, .93 with the continuous change pattern, and .62 with the late change pattern. This child's initial classification would be *early change*. A child with nonverbal scores of .69 at 14 months, .81 at 20 months, and .91 at 24 months had correlations of .91 with the early change pattern, 1.00 with the continuous change pattern, and .82 with the late change pattern. This child's initial classification would be *continuous change.*

The contrast correlations suggested continuous change for a child with scores across a wide range (e.g., .69, .81, and .91) but also for a child with scores across a narrow range (e.g., .80, .81, and .82). To separate meaningful change from random fluctuation, we computed a ratio in which change at the proposed transition was expressed in units of standard deviation. For children categorized as fitting the 1-3-3 pattern, their 14-month score was subtracted from their 20- or 24-month score (whichever was larger), and this difference was divided by the pooled standard deviation for that measure at those two ages. If this ratio was greater than or equal to 1, we were reasonably confident that early change had taken place. For children categorized as fitting the 1-1-3 pattern, their 14- or 20-month score (whichever was smaller) was subtracted from their 24-month score, and this difference was divided by the pooled standard deviation for that measure at those two ages. If this ratio was greater than or equal to 1, we were reasonably confident that late change had taken place. Finally, for children categorized as fitting the 1-2-3 pattern, two ratios were formed: the 14-month score was subtracted from the 20-month score, and the 20-month score was subtracted from the 24-month score. Both were divided by the pooled standard deviation for that measure at those two ages. If both ratios were greater than .50, we were reasonably confident that continuous change had taken place.

Children who did not fit the early change, continuous change, or late change pattern were classified into one of three additional patterns. Some children had anomalous, nonlinear patterns. These patterns were easily detected as a by-product of the contrast correlations—children with a marked nonlinear pattern had one or more negative values. These children, along with those who had one or more missing data points, were considered indeterminate. The children classified as indeterminate represented 22%, 7%, and 2% of the sample at 14, 20, and 24 months, respectively. The remaining children had patterns that suggested no change across age, but inspection of individual scores indicated two types of stability. Some children had three relatively low scores, and some had three relatively high scores. These two distributions had no overlap and could be easily separated by dividing children into groups with means above or below 50% correct. The means for children with no change on the nonverbal construct were all relatively high, and the scatter plot suggested a single distribution. The children classified as not changing represented 11%, 5%, and 4% of the sample at 14, 20, and 24 months, respectively.

To assess the validity of these categorizations, group means (listed in Table B1) were calculated for children classified into each of the patterns of developmental function on each measure. The small standard errors of the mean suggest that the classification method was effective. Moreover, as would be expected, ANOVAs on each of the three dependent variables indicated significant age effects for each group classified as showing change and no age effects for groups classified as showing indeterminate change. Planned contrasts for contiguous ages in the change groups revealed significant effects for 20 versus 24 months in the late change condition, for 14 versus 20 months in the early change condition, and for both contrasts in the continuous change condition. Some groups classified as showing no change did yield significant age effects, but effect sizes were extremely small in comparison to the robust differences for the change groups.

TABLE B1

GROUP MEANS, STANDARD ERRORS OF THE MEAN, AND SAMPLE SIZES FOR CHILDREN CLASSIFIED
INTO EACH CATEGORY OF DEVELOPMENTAL FUNCTION

| VARIABLE AND AGE | CHANGE | | | NO CHANGE | | INDETERMINATE |
	Early	Continuous	Late	Low	High	
Nonverbal:						
14 months	.61	.58	.64		.67	.65
	(.01)	(.01)	(.01)		(.01)	(.01)
20 months	.80	.72	.63		.70	.62
	(.01)	(.01)	(.01)		(.01)	(.01)
24 months	.81	.86	.84		.73	.63
	(.01)	(.01)	(.01)		(.01)	(.01)
N......................	103	125	198		68	140
Verbal expressive:						
14 months	.36	.31	.37	.29	.75	.39
	(.01)	(.01)	(.01)	(.01)	(.01)	(.03)
20 months	.79	.57	.36	.32	.81	.47
	(.01)	(.01)	(.01)	(.01)	(.10)	(.03)
24 months	.80	.82	.76	.39	.84	.40
	(.01)	(.01)	(.01)	(.02)	(.10)	(.03)
N......................	250	199	125	25	3	44
Verbal receptive:						
14 months	.30	.28	.29	.24	.71	.43
	(.01)	(.01)	(.02)	(.02)	(.02)	(.05)
20 months	.70	.53	.32	.30	.75	.58
	(.01)	(.01)	(.02)	(.02)	(.03)	(.07)
24 months	.73	.74	.64	.35	.81	.50
	(.01)	(.01)	(.02)	(.02)	(.02)	(.04)
N......................	312	232	66	11	15	16

NOTE.—Standard errors of the mean are given in parentheses.

REFERENCES

Akaike, H. (1987). Factor analysis and AIC. *Psychometrika, 52,* 317–332.

Anastasi, A. (1976). *Psychological testing* (4th ed.). New York: Macmillan.

Anisfeld, M. (1984). *Language development from birth to three.* Hillsdale, NJ: Erlbaum.

Atkinson, R. C., & Shiffrin, R. M. (1968). Human memory: A proposed system and its control processes. In K. W. Spence & J. T. Spence (Eds.), *The psychology of learning and motivation: Advances in research and theory* (Vol. 2). New York: Academic.

Bates, E., Bretherton, I., & Snyder, L. (1988). *From first words to grammar: Individual differences and dissociable mechanisms.* Cambridge: Cambridge University Press.

Bates, E., & Carnevale, G. F. (1993). New directions in research on language development. *Developmental Review, 13,* 436–470.

Bates, E., Dale, P. S., & Thal, D. (1995). Individual differences and their implications for theories of language development. In P. Fletcher & B. MacWhinney (Eds.), *Handbook of child language.* Oxford: Basil Blackwell.

Bates, E., Marchman, V., Thal, D., Fenson, L., Dale, P., Reznick, J. S., Reilly, J., & Hartung, J. (1994). Developmental and stylistic variation in the composition of early vocabulary. *Journal of Child Language, 21,* 85–123.

Bates, E., Thal, D., & Janowsky, J. S. (1992). Early language development and its neural correlates. In F. Boller & J. Grafman (Ser. Eds.), S. J. Segalowitz & I. Rapin (Vol. Eds.), *Handbook of neuropsychology: Vol. 7. Child neuropsychology.* Amsterdam: Elsevier.

Bayley, N. (1933). *The California First Year Mental Scale.* Berkeley: University of California Press.

Bayley, N. (1969). *Manual for the Bayley Scales of Infant Development.* New York: Psychological Corp.

Bayley, N. (1970). Development of mental abilities. In P. H. Mussen (Ed.), *Carmichael's manual of child psychology* (3d ed., Vol. 1). New York: Wiley.

Bayley, N. (1993). *Manual for the Bayley Scales of Infant Development* (2d ed.). San Antonio, TX: Psychological Corp.

Behrend, D. A. (1988). Overextensions in early language comprehension: Evidence from a signal detection approach. *Journal of Child Language, 15,* 63–75.

Benedict, H. (1979). Early lexical development: Comprehension and production. *Journal of Child Language, 6,* 183–200.

Benson, J. B., Cherny, S. S., Haith, M. M., & Fulker, D. W. (1993). Rapid assessment of infant predictors of adult IQ: Midtwin-midparent analyses. *Developmental Psychology, 29,* 434–447.

Birns, B., & Golden, M. (1972). Prediction of intellectual performance at 3 years from infant tests and personality measures. *Merrill-Palmer Quarterly, 18,* 53–58.

Bloom, L. (1970). *Language development.* Cambridge, MA: MIT Press.

142

Bloom, L. (1973). *One word at a time: The use of single word utterances before syntax*. The Hague: Mouton.

Bornstein, M. H., & Ruddy, M. G. (1984). Infant attention and maternal stimulation: Prediction of cognitive and linguistic development in singletons and twins. In H. Bouma & D. G. Bouwhuis (Eds.), *Attention and performance: 10. Control of language processes*. Hillsdale, NJ: Erlbaum.

Bouchard, T. J., Jr., & McGue, M. (1981). Familial studies of intelligence: A review. *Science, 212,* 1055–1059.

Braungart, J. M., Plomin, R., DeFries, J. C., & Fulker, D. W. (1992). Genetic influence on tester-rated infant temperament as assessed by Bayley's Infant Behavior Record: Non-adoptive and adoptive siblings and twins. *Developmental Psychology, 28,* 40–47.

Broadbent, D. E. (1958). *Perception and communication*. New York: Pergamon.

Bronson, W. C. (1985). Growth in the organization of behavior over the second year of life. *Developmental Psychology, 21,* 108–117.

Brooks, J., & Weinraub, M. (1976). A history of infant intelligence testing. In M. Lewis (Ed.), *Origins of intelligence: Infancy and early childhood*. New York: Plenum.

Brown, R. A. (1973). *A first language: The early stages*. Cambridge, MA: Harvard University Press.

Bruner, J. S. (1973). Organization of early skilled action. *Child Development, 44,* 1–11.

Burchinal, M., & Appelbaum, M. I. (1991). Estimating individual developmental functions: Methods and their assumptions. *Child Development, 62,* 23–43.

Burchinal, M., Lee, M., & Ramey, R. (1989). Type of day care and preschool intellectual development in disadvantaged children. *Child Development, 60,* 128–137.

Burns, W. J., Burns, K. A., & Kabacoff, R. I. (1992). Item and factor analyses of the Bayley Scales of Infant Development. In C. K. Rovee-Collier & L. P. Lipsitt (Eds.), *Advances in infancy research* (Vol. 7). Norwood, NJ: Ablex.

Cardon, L. R. (1991). *PEDIKID*. Boulder: Institute for Behavioral Genetics, University of Colorado.

Cardon, L. R., & Fulker, D. W. (1991). Sources of continuity in infant predictors of later IQ. *Intelligence, 15,* 279–293.

Cardon, L. R., Fulker, D. W., DeFries, J. C., & Plomin, R. (1992). Continuity and change in general cognitive ability from 1 to 7 years of age. *Developmental Psychology, 28,* 64–73.

Carew, J. V. (1980). Experience and the development of intelligence in young children at home and in day care. *Monographs of the Society for Research in Child Development, 45*(6–7, Serial No. 187).

Cattell, P. (1940). *The measurement of intelligence of infants and young children*. New York: Psychological Corp.

Cherny, S. S., DeFries, J. C., & Fulker, D. W. (1992). Multiple regression analysis of twin data: A model-fitting approach. *Behavior Genetics, 22,* 489–497.

Cherny, S. S., Fulker, D. W., Corley, R. P., Plomin, R., & DeFries, J. C. (1994). Continuity and change in infant shyness from 14 to 20 months. *Behavior Genetics, 24,* 365–379.

Cherny, S. S., Fulker, D. W., Emde, R. N., Robinson, J., Corley, R. P., Reznick, J. S., Plomin, R., & DeFries, J. C. (1994). A developmental-genetic analysis of continuity and change in the Bayley Mental Development Index from 14 to 24 months: The MacArthur Longitudinal Twin Study. *Psychological Science, 5,* 354–360.

Colombo, J. (1993). *Infant cognition: Predicting later intellectual functioning*. Newbury Park, CA: Sage.

Colombo, J. (1995). On the neural mechanisms underlying developmental and individual differences in visual fixation in infancy: Two hypotheses. *Developmental Review, 15,* 97–135.

Colombo, J., & Mitchell, D. W. (1990). Individual differences in early visual attention: Fixation time and information processing. In J. Colombo & J. Fagen (Eds.), *Individual differences in infancy: Reliability, stability, prediction.* Hillsdale, NJ: Erlbaum.

Conway, D., Lytton, H., & Pysh, F. (1980). Twin-singleton language differences. *Canadian Journal of Behavioral Science, 12,* 264–271.

Cowan, N. (1988). Evolving conceptions of memory storage, selective attention, and their mutual constraints within the human information processing system. *Psychological Bulletin, 104,* 163–191.

Cronbach, L. J. (1951). Coefficient alpha and the internal structure of tests. *Psychometrika, 16,* 297–234.

Cronbach, L. J. (1957). The two disciplines of scientific psychology. *American Psychologist, 12,* 671–684.

Cronbach, L. J. (1967). Year-to-year correlations of mental tests: A review of the Hofstaetter analysis. *Child Development, 38,* 283–289.

Cyphers, L. H., Phillips, K., Fulker, D. W., & Mrazek, D. A. (1990). Twin temperament during the transition from infancy to early childhood. *Journal of the American Academy of Child and Adolescent Psychiatry, 29,* 392–397.

Dale, P. S., Bates, E., Reznick, J. S., & Morisset, C. (1989). The validity of a parent report instrument of child language at 20 months. *Journal of Child Language, 16,* 239–249.

Darwin, C. (1859). *On the origin of species by means of natural selection; or, The preservation of favoured races in the struggle for life.* New York: Appleton.

Davies, D. R., Jones, D. M., & Taylor, A. (1984). Selective- and sustained-attention tasks: Individual and group differences. In R. Parasuraman & D. R. Davies (Eds.), *Varieties of attention.* Orlando, FL: Academic.

Dawson, G., & Fischer, K. W. (Eds.). (1994). *Human behavior and the developing brain.* New York: Guilford.

Day, E. J. (1932). The development of language in twins: 1. A comparison of twins and single children. *Child Development, 3,* 179–199.

DeFries, J. C. (1985). Colorado Reading Project. In D. B. Gray & J. F. Kavanagh (Eds.), *Biobehavioral measures of dyslexia.* Parkton, MD: York.

DeFries, J. C., & Fulker, D. W. (1988). Multiple regression analysis of twin data: Etiology of deviant score versus individual differences. *Acta Geneticae Medicae et Gemeologiae, 37,* 205–216.

DeFries, J. C., Plomin, R., & LaBuda, M. C. (1987). Genetic stability of cognitive development from childhood to adulthood. *Developmental Psychology, 23,* 4–12.

Detterman, D. K. (1979). A job half done: The road to intelligence testing in the year 2000. *Intelligence, 3,* 295–306.

Diamond, A. (1985). Development of the ability to use recall to guide action, as indicated by infants' performance on AB. *Child Development, 56,* 868–883.

Diamond, A. (1990). Developmental time course in human infants and infant monkeys, and the neural bases, of inhibitory control in reaching. In A. Diamond (Ed.), *The development and neural bases of higher cognitive functions.* New York: New York Academy of Sciences.

Diamond, A., & Doar, B. (1989). The performance of human infants on a measure of frontal cortex function, the delayed response task. *Developmental Psychobiology, 22,* 271–294.

Diamond, A., Towle, C., & Boyer, K. (1994). Young children's performance on a task sensitive to the memory functions of the medial temporal lobe in adults—the delayed nonmatching-to-sample task—reveals problems that are due to non-memory-related task demands. *Behavioral Neuroscience, 108,* 659–680.

DiLalla, L. F., Kagan, J., & Reznick, J. S. (1994). Genetic etiology of behavioral inhibition among two-year-old children. *Infant Behavior and Development, 17,* 401–408.

DiLalla, L. F., Thompson, L. A., Plomin, R., Phillips, K., Fagan, J. F., Haith, M. H., Cyphers,

L. H., & Fulker, D. W. (1990). Infant predictors of preschool and adult IQ: A study of infant twins and their parents. *Developmental Psychology, 26,* 759–769.

Dodd, B., & McEvoy, S. (1994). Twin language or phonological disorder? *Journal of Child Language, 21,* 273–289.

Dunn, J., & Plomin, R. (1990). *Separate lives: Why children in the same family are so different.* New York: Basic.

Dunst, C. J. (1978). The structure of infant intelligence: An historical overview. *Intelligence, 2,* 381–391.

Eaves, L. J., Long, J., & Heath, A. C. (1986). A theory of developmental change in quantitative phenotypes applied to cognitive development. *Behavior Genetics, 16,* 143–162.

Emde, R., Campos, J., Corley, R., DeFries, J., Fulker, D., Kagan, J., Plomin, R., Reznick, J. S., Robinson, J., & Zahn-Waxler, C. (1992). Temperament, emotion, and cognition at 14 months: The MacArthur Longitudinal Twin Study. *Child Development, 63,* 1437–1455.

Emmerich, W. (1964). Continuity and stability in early social development. *Child Development, 35,* 311–332.

Fagan, J. F., & McGrath, S. K. (1981). Infant recognition memory and later intelligence. *Intelligence, 5,* 121–130.

Fenson, L., Dale, P. S., Reznick, J. S., Bates, E., Thal, D. J., & Pethick, S. J. (1994). Variability in early communicative development. *Monographs of the Society for Research in Child Development, 59*(5, Serial No. 242).

Fenson, L., Dale, P., Reznick, J. S., Thal, D., Bates, E., Hartung, J. P., Pethick, S., & Reilly, J. S. (1993). *The MacArthur Communicative Development Inventories: User's guide and technical manual.* San Diego: Singular.

Fifer, W. P. (1987). Neonatal preference for mother's voice. In N. A. Krasnegor, E. M. Blass, M. A. Hofer, & W. P. Smotherman (Eds.), *Perinatal development: A psychobiological perspective.* New York: Academic.

Fischer, K. W. (1980). A theory of cognitive development: The control and construction of hierarchies of skills. *Psychological Review, 87,* 477–531.

Fox, N., Kagan, J., & Weiskopf, S. (1979). The growth of memory during infancy. *Genetic Psychology Monographs, 99,* 91–130.

Fremgen, A., & Fay, D. (1980). Overextensions in production and comprehension: A methodological clarification. *Journal of Child Language, 7,* 205–211.

Fulker, D. W., Cherny, S. S., & Cardon, L. R. (1993). Continuity and change in cognitive development. In R. Plomin & G. E. McClearn (Eds.), *Nature, nurture, and psychology.* Washington, DC: American Psychological Association.

Fulker, D. W., DeFries, J. C., & Plomin, R. (1988). Genetic influences on general mental ability increases between infancy and middle childhood. *Nature, 336,* 767–769.

Galton, F. (1883). *Inquiries into human faculty and its development.* London: Macmillan.

Galton, F. (1962). *Hereditary genius: An inquiry into its laws and consequences.* Cleveland: World Publishing Co. (Original work published 1869)

Gardner, H. (1983). *Frames of mind: The theory of multiple intelligences.* New York: Basic.

Gesell, A. (1925). *The mental growth of the preschool child.* New York: Macmillan.

Gesell, A. (1928). *Infancy and human growth.* New York: Macmillan.

Gibson, K. R., & Petersen, A. C. (Eds.). (1991). *Brain maturation and cognitive development: Comparative and cross-cultural perspectives.* New York: Aldine De Gruyter.

Goldfarb, W. (1943). Infant rearing and problem behavior. *American Journal of Orthopsychiatry, 13,* 249–265.

Goldfield, B. A. (1993). Noun bias in maternal speech to one-year-olds. *Journal of Child Language, 20,* 85–99.

Goldfield, B. A., & Reznick, J. S. (1990). Early lexical acquisition: Rate, content, and the vocabulary spurt. *Journal of Child Language,* **17,** 171–183.

Goldfield, E. C. (1995). *Emergent forms: Origins and early development of human action and perception.* New York: Oxford.

Goldsmith, H. H. (1993). Nature-nurture issues in the behavioral genetics context: Overcoming barriers to communication. In R. Plomin & G. E. McClearn (Eds.), *Nature, nurture, and psychology.* Washington, DC: American Psychological Association.

Golinkoff, G. M., Hirsh-Pasek, K., Cauley, K. M., & Gordon, L. (1987). The eyes have it: Lexical and syntactic comprehension in a new paradigm. *Journal of Child Language,* **14,** 23–45.

Goodenough, F. L. (1939). Look to the evidence: A critique of recent experiments on raising the IQ. *Education Methods,* **19,** 73–79.

Gopnik, A., & Meltzoff, A. (1987). The development of categorization in the second year and its relation to other cognitive and linguistic developments. *Child Development,* **58,** 1523–1531.

Griffiths, R. (1954). *The abilities of babies: A study in mental measurement.* New York: McGraw-Hill.

Guilford, J. P. (1967). *The nature of human intelligence.* New York: McGraw-Hill.

Gyurke, J. S., Lynch, S. J., Lagasse, L., & Lipsitt, L. P. (1992). Speeded items: What do they tell us about an infant's performance? In C. K. Rovee-Collier & L. P. Lipsitt (Eds.), *Advances in infancy research* (Vol. 7). Norwood, NJ: Ablex.

Hampson, J., & Nelson, K. (1993). The relation of maternal language to variation in rate and style of language acquisition. *Journal of Child Language,* **20,** 313–342.

Hardy-Brown, K., & Plomin, R. (1985). Infant communicative development: Evidence from adoptive and biological families for genetic and environmental influences on rate differences. *Developmental Psychology,* **21,** 378–385.

Hardy-Brown, K., Plomin, R., & DeFries, J. C. (1981). Genetic and environmental influences on the rate of communicative development in the first year of life. *Developmental Psychology,* **17,** 704–717.

Harris, M., Yeeles, C., Chasin, J., & Oakley, Y. (1995). Symmetries and asymmetries in early lexical comprehension and production. *Journal of Child Language,* **22,** 1–18.

Hedrick, D. L., Prather, E. M., & Tobin, A. R. (1975). *Sequenced Inventory of Communication Development.* Seattle: University of Washington Press.

Hirsh-Pasek, K., Golinkoff, G. M., Fletcher, A., deGaspe Beaubien, F., & Cauley, K. (1985, October). *In the beginning: One-word speakers comprehend word order.* Paper presented at the Boston Child Language Conference, Boston.

Hoff-Ginsberg, E. (1991). Mother-child conversation in different social classes and communicative settings. *Child Development,* **62,** 782–796.

Hoff-Ginsberg, E. (1994). Influences of mother and child on maternal talkativeness. *Discourse Processes,* **18,** 105–117.

Hofstadter, M., & Reznick, J. S. (1996). Response modality affects human infant delayed-response performance. *Child Development,* **67,** 646–658.

Hofstaetter, P. R. (1954). The changing composition of "intelligence": A study in T-technique. *Journal of Genetic Psychology,* **85,** 159–164.

Howie, P. M. (1981). Concordance for stuttering in monozygotic and dizygotic twin pairs. *Journal of Speech and Hearing Research,* **24,** 317–321.

Humphreys, L. G., & Davey, T. C. (1988). Continuity in intellectual growth from 12 months to 9 years. *Intelligence,* **12,** 183–197.

Hunter, W. S. (1913). The delayed reaction in animals and children. *Behavior Monographs,* **2,** 1–86.

Huttenlocher, J., Haight, W., Bryk, A., Seltzer, M., & Lyons, T. (1991). Early vocabulary growth: Relation to language input and gender. *Developmental Psychology, 27,* 236–248.

Huttenlocher, P. R. (1990). Morphometric study of human cerebral cortex development. *Neuropsychologia, 28,* 517–527.

Ingram, D. (1974). The relationship between comprehension and production. In R. L. Schiefelbusch & L. L. Lloyd (Eds.), *Language perspectives: Acquisition, retardation, and intervention.* Baltimore: University Park Press.

Joreskog, K. G., & Sorbom, D. (1989). *LISREL 7: A guide to the program and applications* (2d ed.). Chicago: SPSS.

Kagan, J. (1981). *The second year.* Cambridge, MA: Harvard University Press.

Kagan, J., & Hamburg, M. (1981). The enhancement of memory in the first year. *Journal of Genetic Psychology, 138,* 3–14.

Kagan, J., Kearsley, R. B., & Zelazo, P. R. (1978). *Infancy: Its place in human development.* Cambridge, MA: Harvard University Press.

Kendler, H. H. (1987). *Historical foundations of modern psychology.* Chicago: Dorsey.

Kessen, W. (1984). Introduction: The end of the age of development. In R. J. Sternberg (Ed.), *Mechanisms of cognitive development.* New York: W. H. Freeman.

Kimble, G. A. (1993). Evolution of the nature-nurture issue in the history of psychology. In R. Plomin & G. E. McClearn (Eds.), *Nature, nurture, and psychology.* Washington, DC: American Psychological Association.

Kohen-Raz, R. (1967). Scalogram analysis of some developmental sequences of infant behavior as measured by the Bayley Infant Scale of Mental Development. *Genetic Psychology Monographs, 76,* 3–21.

Kopp, C. B., & Vaughn, B. E. (1982). Sustained attention during exploratory manipulation as a predictor of cognitive competence in preterm infants. *Child Development, 53,* 174–182.

Kurnit, D. M., Layton, W. M., & Matthysse, S. (1987). Genetics, chance, and morphogenesis. *American Journal of Human Genetics, 41,* 979–995.

Leonard, L. B., Newhoff, M., & Fey, M. E. (1980). Some instances of word usage in the absence of comprehension. *Journal of Child Language, 7,* 189–196.

Leonard, L. B., Newhoff, M., & Mesalam, L. (1980). Individual differences in early child phonology. *Applied Psycholinguistics, 1,* 7–30.

Lewis, B. A., Ekelman, B. L., & Aram, D. M. (1989). A family study of severe phonological disorders. *Journal of Speech and Hearing Research, 23,* 713–724.

Lewis, B. A., & Thompson, L. A. (1992). A study of developmental speech and language disorders in twins. *Journal of Speech and Hearing Research, 35,* 1086–1094.

Lewis, M., & Brooks-Gunn, J. (1979). *Social cognition and the acquisition of self.* New York: Plenum.

Lewis, M., Jaskir, J., & Enright, M. K. (1986). The development of mental abilities in infancy. *Intelligence, 10,* 331–354.

Lieven, E. M. (1978). Conversations between mothers and young children: Individual differences and their possible implications for the study of language learning. In N. Waterson & C. Snow (Eds.), *The development of communication: Social and pragmatic factors in language acquisition.* New York: Wiley.

Locke, J. L. (1990). Structure and stimulation in the ontogeny of spoken language. *Developmental Psychobiology, 23,* 621–643.

Locke, J. L., & Mather, P. L. (1989). Genetic factors in the ontogeny of spoken language: Evidence from monozygotic and dizygotic twins. *Journal of Child Language, 16,* 553–559.

Loehlin, J. C. (1996). The Cholesky approach: A cautionary note. *Behavior Genetics, 26,* 65–69.

Loehlin, J. C., & Nichols, R. C. (1976). *Heredity, environment and personality*. Austin: University of Texas Press.

Lykken, D. T., McGue, M., & Tellegen, A. (1987). Recruitment bias in twin research: The rule of two-thirds reconsidered. *Behavior Genetics, 17,* 343–362.

Lykken, D. T., McGue, M., Tellegen, A., & Bouchard, T. J., Jr. (1992). Emergenesis: Genetic traits that may not run in families. *American Psychologist, 47,* 1565–1577.

Lytton, H., Conway, D., & Sauve, R. (1977). The impact of twinship on parent-child interaction. *Journal of Personality and Social Psychology, 25,* 97–107.

Macaulay, R. (1978). The myth of female superiority in language. *Journal of Child Language, 5,* 353–363.

MacGillivray, L., Nylander, P. P. S., & Corney, G. (1975). *Human multiple reproduction*. London: Saunders.

Malmstrom, P. M., & Silva, M. N. (1986). Twin talk: Manifestations of twin status in the speech of toddlers. *Journal of Child Language, 13,* 293–304.

Matheny, A. P., Jr. (1980). Bayley's Infant Behavior Record: Behavioral components and twin analyses. *Child Development, 51,* 1157–1167.

Matheny, A. P., Jr. (1983). A longitudinal twin study of stability of components from Bayley's Infant Behavior Record. *Child Development, 54,* 356–360.

Matheny, A. P., Jr. (1989). Temperament and cognition: Relations between temperament and mental test scores. In G. A. Kohnstamm, J. E. Bates, & M. K. Rothbard (Eds.), *Temperament in childhood*. New York: Wiley.

Matheny, A. P., Jr., & Bruggemann, C. (1972). Articulation proficiency in twins and singletons from families of twins. *Journal of Speech and Hearing Research, 15,* 845–851.

Matheny, A. P., Jr., Dolan, A. B., & Wilson, R. S. (1976). Twins: Within-pair similarity on Bayley's Infant Behavior Record. *Journal of Genetic Psychology, 128,* 263–270.

Matheny, A. P., Jr., Wilson, R. S., & Dolan, A. B. (1976). Relations between twins' similarity of appearance and behavioral similarity: Testing an assumption. *Behavior Genetics, 6,* 343–351.

Mather, P. L., & Black, K. N. (1984). Hereditary and environmental influences on preschool twins' language skills. *Developmental Psychology, 20,* 303–308.

Mayes, L. C., & Bornstein, M. H. (1995). Infant information-processing performance and maternal education. *Early Development and Parenting, 4,* 91–96.

McCall, R. B. (1981). Nature-nurture and the two realms of development: A proposed integration with respect to mental development. *Child Development, 52,* 1–12.

McCall, R. B. (1994). What process mediates predictions of childhood IQ from infant habituation and recognition memory? Speculations on the roles of inhibition and rate of information processing. *Intelligence, 18,* 107–125.

McCall, R. B., Appelbaum, M. I., & Hogarty, P. S. (1973). Developmental changes in mental performance. *Monographs of the Society for Research in Child Development, 38*(3, Serial No. 150).

McCall, R. B., & Carriger, M. S. (1993). A meta-analysis of infant habituation and recognition memory performance as predictors of later IQ. *Child Development, 64,* 57–79.

McCall, R. B., Eichorn, D. H., & Hogarty, P. S. (1977). Transitions in early mental development. *Monographs of the Society for Research in Child Development, 42*(3, Serial No. 171).

McCarthy, D. (1954). Language development in children. In L. Carmichael (Ed.), *Manual of child psychology*. New York: Wiley.

McCartney, K., Harris, M. J., & Bernieri, F. (1990). Growing up and growing apart: A developmental meta-analysis of twin studies. *Psychological Bulletin, 107,* 226–237.

McGue, M., Bouchard, T. J., Jr., Iacono, W. G., & Lykken, D. T. (1993). Behavioral genetics of cognitive ability: A life-span perspective. In R. Plomin & G. E. McClearn (Eds.), *Nature, nurture, and psychology*. Washington, DC: American Psychological Association.

Meltzoff, A. N. (1990). Towards a developmental cognitive science. In A. Diamond (Ed.), *The development and neural bases of higher cognitive functions.* New York: New York Academy of Sciences.

Meltzoff, A. N., & Gopnik, A. (1989). On linking nonverbal imitation, representation, and language learning in the first two years of life. In G. E. Speidel & K. E. Nelson (Eds.), *The many faces of imitation in language learning.* New York: Springer.

Merenstein, G. B., Kaplan, D. W., & Rosenberg, A. A. (1991). *Silver, Kempe, Bruyn and Fulginiti's handbook of pediatrics* (16th ed.). Norwalk, CT: Appleton & Lange.

Minde, K., Carter, C., Goldberg, S., & Jeffers, D. (1990). Maternal preference between premature twins up to age four. *Journal of the American Academy of Child and Adolescent Psychiatry,* **29,** 367–374.

Mittler, P. (1969). Genetic aspects of psycholinguistic abilities. *Journal of Child Psychology and Psychiatry,* **10,** 165–176.

Molenaar, P. C. M., Boomsma, D. I., & Dolan, C. V. (1993). A third source of developmental differences. *Behavioral Genetics,* **23,** 519–524.

Morissette, P., Ricard, M., & Decarie, T. G. (1995). Joint visual attention and pointing in infancy: A longitudinal study of comprehension. *British Journal of Developmental Psychology,* **13,** 163–175.

Munsinger, H., & Douglass, A., II. (1976). The syntactic abilities of identical twins, fraternal twins, and their siblings. *Child Development,* **47,** 40–50.

Naeye, R. L., Benirschke, K., Hagstrom, J. W. C., & Marcus, C. C. (1966). Intrauterine growth of twins as estimated from live birth weight data. *Pediatrics,* **37,** 409–416.

Naigles, L. (1990). Children use syntax to learn verb meanings. *Journal of Child Language,* **17,** 357–374.

Naigles, L. G., & Gelman, S. A. (1995). Overextensions in comprehension and production revisited: Preferential-looking in a study of dog, cat, and cow. *Journal of Child Language,* **22,** 19–46.

Neale, M. C. (1994). *Mx: Statistical modeling* (2d ed.). (Available from the Department of Psychiatry, Medical College of Virginia, Virginia Commonwealth University, Box 710 MCV, Richmond VA 23298-0710)

Neale, M. C., & Cardon, L. R. (1992). *Methodology for genetic studies of twins and families* (NATO ASI Series). Norwell, MA: Kluwer Academic.

Neisser, U., Boodoo, G., Bouchard, T. J., Jr., Boykin, A. W., Brody, N., Ceci, S. J., Halpern, D. F., Loehlin, J. C., Perloff, R., Sternberg, R. J., & Urbina, S. (1996). Intelligence: Knowns and unknowns. *American Psychologist,* **51,** 77–101.

Nelson, K. (1973). Structure and strategy in learning to talk. *Monographs of the Society for Research in Child Development,* **38**(1–2, Serial No. 149).

Nelson, K., & Bonvillian, J. (1973). Concepts and words in the 18-month-old: Acquiring concept names under controlled conditions. *Cognition,* **2,** 435–450.

Nichols, P. L., & Broman, S. H. (1974). Familial resemblance in infant mental development. *Developmental Psychology,* **10,** 442–446.

Nichols, R. C., & Bilbro, W. C. (1966). The diagnosis of twin zygosity. *Acta Geneticae Medicae et Statistica,* **16,** 265–275.

Overman, W. H. (1990). Performance on traditional matching to sample, non–matching to sample, and object discrimination tasks by 12- to 32-month-old children. In A. Diamond (Ed.), *The development and neural bases of higher cognitive functions.* New York: New York Academy of Sciences.

Oviatt, S. L. (1980). The emerging ability to comprehend language: An experimental approach. *Child Development,* **51,** 97–106.

Oviatt, S. L. (1982). Inferring what words mean: Early development in infants' comprehension of common object names. *Child Development,* **53,** 274–277.

Pennington, B. F., & Smith, S. D. (1983). Genetic influences on learning disabilities and speech and language disorders. *Child Development, 54,* 369–387.

Petrill, S. A., & Thompson, L. A. (1993). The phenotypic and genetic relationships among measures of cognitive ability, temperament, and scholastic achievement. *Behavior Genetics, 23,* 511–518.

Piaget, J. (1952). *The origins of intelligence in children.* New York: Norton.

Plomin, R. (1986). *Development, genetics, and psychology.* Hillsdale, NJ: Erlbaum.

Plomin, R. (1988). The nature and nurture of cognitive abilities. In R. Sternberg (Ed.), *Advances in the psychology of human intelligence* (Vol. 4). Norwood, NJ: Ablex.

Plomin, R., Campos, J., Corley, R., Emde, R. N., Fulker, D. W., Kagan, J., Reznick, J. S., Robinson, J., Zahn-Waxler, C., & DeFries, J. C. (1990). Individual differences during the second year of life: The MacArthur Longitudinal Twin Study. In J. Colombo & J. W. Fagan (Eds.) *Individual differences in infancy: Reliability, stability, prediction.* Hillsdale, NJ: Erlbaum.

Plomin, R., & Daniels, D. (1987). Why are children in the same family so different? *Behavioral and Brain Sciences, 10,* 1–16.

Plomin, R., & DeFries, J. C. (1985). *Origins of individual difference in infancy: The Colorado Adoption Project.* New York: Academic.

Plomin, R., DeFries, J. C., & Fulker, D. W. (1988). *Nature and nurture during infancy and early childhood.* Cambridge: Cambridge University Press.

Plomin, R., DeFries, J. C., & McClearn, G. E. (1990). *Behavioral genetics: A primer* (2d ed.). New York: Freeman.

Plomin, R., Emde, R. N., Braungart, J. M., Campos, J., Corley, R., Fulker, D. W., Kagan, J., Reznick, J. S., Robinson, J., Zahn-Waxler, C., & DeFries, J. C. (1993). Genetic change and continuity from fourteen to twenty months: The MacArthur Longitudinal Twin Study. *Child Development, 64,* 1354–1376.

Posner, M. I., & Petersen, S. E. (1990). The attention system of the human brain. *Annual Review of Neuroscience, 13,* 25–42.

Quartz, S. R., & Sejnowski, T. J. (in press). The neural basis of cognitive development: A constructivist manifesto. *Behavioral and Brain Sciences.*

Rescorla, L. A. (1984). Individual differences in early language development and their predictive significance. *Acta Paedologica, 1,* 97–116.

Reznick, J. S. (1982). *The development of perceptual and lexical categories in the human infant.* Unpublished doctoral dissertation, University of Colorado, Boulder.

Reznick, J. S. (1990). Visual preference as a test of infant word comprehension. *Applied Psycholinguistics, 11,* 145–165.

Reznick, J. S., & Goldfield, B. A. (1992). Rapid change in lexical development in comprehension and production. *Developmental Psychology, 28,* 406–413.

Reznick, J. S., & Goldfield, B. A. (1994). Diary versus representative checklist assessment of productive vocabulary. *Journal of Child Language, 21,* 465–472.

Robin, M., Josse, D., Casati, I., Kherova, H., & Tourette, C. (1993). La gémellisation de l'environment physique des jumeaux. *Attitudes et Pratiques Maternelles Enfance, 47,* 393–406.

Robinson, J. L., & Biringen, Z. (1995). Gender and emerging autonomy in development. *Psychoanalytic Inquiry, 15,* 60–74.

Robinson, J. L., Kagan, J., Reznick, J. S., & Corley, R. (1992). The heritability of inhibited and uninhibited behavior: A twin study. *Developmental Psychology, 28,* 1030–1037.

Robinson, J. L., Zahn-Waxler, C., & Emde, R. N. (1994). Patterns of development in early empathic behavior: Environmental and child constitutional influences. *Social Development, 3,* 125–145.

Rose, S. A., & Feldman, J. F. (1995). Prediction of IQ and specific cognitive abilities at 11 years from infancy measures. *Developmental Psychology*, **31**, 685–696.

Rose, S. A., Feldman, J. F., Wallace, I. F., & Cohen, P. (1991). Language: A partial link between infant attention and later intelligence. *Developmental Psychology*, **27**, 798–805.

Rovee-Collier, C. (1990). The "memory system" of prelinguistic infants. In A. Diamond (Ed.), *The development and neural bases of higher cognitive functions*. New York: New York Academy of Sciences.

Ruff, H. A. (1990). Individual differences in sustained attention during infancy. In J. Colombo & J. Fagen (Eds.), *Individual differences in infancy: Reliability, stability, prediction*. Hillsdale, NJ: Erlbaum.

Ruff, H. A., & Rothbart, M. K. (1996). *Attention in early development: Themes and variations*. New York: Oxford.

Sattler, J. M. (1990). *Assessment of children* (3d ed.). San Diego: Sattler.

Saudino, K. J., & Eaton, W. O. (1995). Continuity and change in objectively assessed temperament: A longitudinal twin study of activity level. *British Journal of Developmental Psychology*, **13**, 81–95.

Savic, S. (1979). Mother-child verbal interaction: The functioning of completions in the twin situation. *Journal of Child Language*, **6**, 153–158.

Savic, S. (1980). *How twins learn to talk*. New York: Academic.

Scarr, S., & McCartney, K. (1983). How people make their own environments: A theory of genotype → environment effects. *Child Development*, **54**, 424–435.

Schmidt, F. L. (1996). Statistical significance testing and cumulative knowledge in psychology: Implications for training of researchers. *Psychological Methods*, **1**, 115–129.

Shatz, M. (1994). *A toddler's life: Becoming a person*. New York: Oxford University Press.

Shiono, P. H., & Behrman, R. E. (1995). Low birth weight: Analysis and recommendations. *The Future of Children*, **5**, 4–18.

Shore, C. M. (1995). *Individual differences in language development*. Thousand Oaks, CA: Sage.

Siegel, L. S. (1981). Infant tests as predictors of cognitive and language development at two years. *Child Development*, **52**, 545–557.

Siegel, S. (1956). *Nonparametric statistics for the behavioral sciences*. New York: McGraw-Hill.

Sigman, M., Cohen, S. E., Beckwith, L., & Topinka, C. (1987). Task persistence in 2-year-old preterm infants in relation to subsequent attentiveness and intelligence. *Infant Behavior and Development*, **10**, 295–305.

Simpson, B. R. (1939). The wandering IQ; is it time to settle down? *Journal of Psychology*, **7**, 351–367.

Sincoff, J. B., & Sternberg, R. J. (1987). Two faces of verbal ability. *Intelligence*, **11**, 263–276.

Slater, A. (1994). Individual differences in infancy and later IQ. *Journal of Child Psychology and Psychiatry and Allied Disciplines*, **36**, 69–112.

Slomkowski, C. L., Nelson, K., Dunn, J., & Plomin, R. (1992). Temperament and language: Relations from toddlerhood to middle childhood. *Developmental Psychology*, **28**, 1090–1095.

Smith, L. B., & Thelen, E. (Eds.). (1993). *A dynamic systems approach to development: Applications*. Cambridge, MA: MIT Press.

Smolak, L., & Weinraub, M. (1983). Maternal speech: Strategy or response? *Journal of Child Language*, **10**, 369–380.

Spearman, C. (1904). General intelligence objectively determined and measured. *American Journal of Psychology*, **14**, 201–293.

Spreen, O., & Strauss, E. (1991). *A compendium of neuropsychological tests: Administration, norms, and commentary*. New York: Oxford.

Stafford, L. (1987). Maternal input to twin and singleton children: Implications for language acquisition. *Human Communication Research,* **13,** 429–462.

Stern, W. (1914). *The psychological methods of testing intelligence.* Baltimore: Warwick & York.

Sternberg, R. J. (1977). *Intelligence, information processing, and analogical reasoning: The componential analysis of human abilities.* Hillsdale, NJ: Erlbaum.

Stott, L., & Ball, R. (1965). Infant and preschool mental tests: Review and evaluation. *Monographs of the Society for Research in Child Development,* **30**(3, Serial No. 101).

Tallal, P., Ross, R., & Curtiss, S. (1989). Familial aggregation in specific language impairment. *Journal of Speech and Hearing Disorders,* **54,** 167–173.

Tamis-LeMonda, C. S., & Bornstein, M. H. (1989). Habituation and maternal encouragement of attention in infancy as predictors of toddler language, play, and representational competence. *Child Development,* **60,** 738–751.

Tamis-LeMonda, C. S., & Bornstein, M. H. (1990). Language, play, and attention at one year. *Infant Behavior and Development,* **13,** 85–98.

Tanaka, J. S. (1993). Multifaceted conceptions of fit in structural equation models. In K. A. Bollen & J. S. Long (Eds.), *Testing structural equation models.* Newbury Park, CA: Sage.

Terman, L. M. (1918). Vocabulary test as a measure of intelligence. *Journal of Educational Psychology,* **9,** 452–466.

Thal, D., & Bates, E. (1988). Language and gesture in late talkers. *Journal of Speech and Hearing Research,* **31,** 115–123.

Thal, D., Tobias, S., & Morrison, D. (1991). Language and gesture in late talkers: A one-year follow-up. *Journal of Speech and Hearing Research,* **34,** 604–612.

Thelen, E., & Smith, L. B. (1994). *A dynamic systems approach to the development of cognition and action.* Cambridge, MA: MIT Press.

Thomas, D. C., Campos, J. J., Shucard, D. W., Ramsey, D., & Shucard, J. (1981). Semantic comprehension in infancy: A signal detection analysis. *Child Development,* **52,** 798–803.

Thompson, G. A. (1919). On the cause of hierarchical order among correlation coefficients. *Proceedings of the Royal Society of London: Series A. Mathematical and Physical Sciences,* **95,** 400–408.

Thompson, J. R., & Chapman, R. S. (1977). Who is "Daddy" revisited: The status of two-year-olds' over-extended words in use and comprehension. *Journal of Child Language,* **4,** 359–375.

Thompson, L. A., Fagan, J. F., & Fulker, D. W. (1991). Longitudinal prediction of specific cognitive abilities from infant novelty preference. *Child Development,* **62,** 530–538.

Thompson, L. A., & Plomin, R. (1988). The Sequenced Inventory of Communication Development: An adoption study of two- and three-year-olds. *International Journal of Behavioral Development,* **11,** 219–231.

Thorndike, E. (1914). *Educational psychology* (Vol. 3). New York: Columbia University Press.

Thurstone, L. L. (1938). *Primary mental abilities.* Chicago: University of Chicago Press.

Tomasello, M., Mannle, S., & Kruger, A. (1986). Linguistic environment of 1- to 2-year-old twins. *Developmental Psychology,* **22,** 169–176.

Tourette, C., Robin, M., & Josse, D. (1988). Les pratiques éducatives des mères de jumeaux: Une investigation par l'analyse factorielle des correspondences. *L'Anée Psychologique,* **88,** 545–561.

Tourette, C., Robin, M., & Josse, D. (1989). Treating twins as individuals: Maternal educative practices. *European Journal of Psychology and Education,* **4,** 269–283.

Turkheimer, E. (1991). Individual and group differences in adoption studies of IQ. *Psychological Bulletin,* **110,** 392–405.

Uzgiris, I. C. (1976). Organization of sensorimotor intelligence. In M. Lewis (Ed.), *Origins of intelligence.* New York: Plenum.

Uzgiris, I. C., & Hunt, J. McV. (1975). *Assessment in infancy: Ordinal scales of psychological development.* Urbana: University of Illinois Press.

Vandenberg, S. G. (1976). Twin studies. In A. R. Kaplan (Ed.), *Human behavior genetics.* Springfield, IL: Charles C. Thomas.

Vigilant, L., Stoneking, M., Harpending, H., Hawkes, K., & Wilson, A. C. (1991). African populations and the evolution of human mitochondrial DNA. *Science, 253,* 1503–1507.

Vygotsky, L. S. (1962). *Thought and language.* Cambridge, MA: MIT Press.

Wahlsten, D. (1994). The intelligence of heritability. *Canadian Psychology, 35,* 244–260.

Warm, J. S. (1984). An introduction to vigilance. In J. S. Warm (Ed.), *Sustained attention in human performance.* Chichester: Wiley.

Wechsler, D. (1949). *Manual, Wechsler Intelligence Scale for Children.* New York: Psychological Corp.

Wellman, B. L. (1932). Some new bases for interpretation of the IQ. *Journal of Genetic Psychology, 41,* 116–126.

Williams, L. J., & Holohan, P. J. (1994). Parsimony-based fit indices for multiple-indicator models: Do they work? *Structural Equation Modeling, 1,* 161–189.

Wilson, R. S. (1977). Mental development in twins. In A. Oliverio (Ed.), *Genetics, environment, and intelligence.* Alphen aan den Rijn: Elsevier.

Wilson, R. S. (1983). The Louisville Twin Study: Developmental synchronies in behavior. *Child Development, 54,* 298–316.

Wilson, R. S. (1985). Risk and resilience in early mental development. *Developmental Psychology, 21,* 795–805.

Wilson, R. S., & Harpring, E. B. (1972). Mental and motor development in infant twins. *Developmental Psychology, 7,* 277–287.

Wilson, S. M., Corley, R. P., Fulker, D. W., & Reznick, J. S. (1996). *Experimental assessment of specific cognitive abilities during the second year of life.* Unpublished manuscript, Institute for Behavioral Genetics, University of Colorado, Boulder.

Wohlwill, J. F. (1973). *The study of behavioral development.* New York: Academic.

Yarrow, L. J., Rubenstein, J. L., & Pedersen, F. A. (1975). *Infant and environment: Early cognitive and motivational development.* New York: Wiley.

Zahn-Waxler, C., Robinson, J. L., & Emde, R. N. (1992). The development of empathy in twins. *Developmental Psychology, 28,* 1038–1047.

ACKNOWLEDGMENTS

The results reported here emerged through collaboration among a group of investigators, including John C. DeFries, Robert N. Emde, and David Fulker at the University of Colorado; Joseph J. Campos at the University of California, Berkeley; Jerome Kagan at Harvard University; Robert Plomin at the Institute of Psychiatry, London; and Carolyn Zahn-Waxler at the National Institute of Mental Health. This research was supported by the John D. and Catherine T. MacArthur Foundation through its Research Network on Early Childhood Transitions.

We thank the families who contributed their time and effort as well as the many research assistants at the University of Colorado, Harvard University, Yale University, and the Pennsylvania State University who were involved in data collection, behavior coding, and data management.

We thank the following colleagues for their editorial suggestions: Nancy Apfel, Elizabeth Bates, Janette Benson, Alice Carter, Philip Dale, John DeFries, Lisabeth DiLalla, Larry Fenson, Beverly Goldfield, Jerome Kagan, William Kessen, David Moore, Letitia Naigles, David Pauls, Robert Plomin, Keith Whitfield, and Philip D. Zelazo.

Correspondence concerning this *Monograph* should be addressed to J. Steven Reznick, Psychology Department, Box 208205, New Haven CT 06520-8205, or reznick@yale.edu.

INFANTS' COGNITIVE DEVELOPMENT:
TRAJECTORY AND SEGUE

Adam P. Matheny Jr.

During recent years, developmental psychology has undergone a revision regarding potential biological contributions to the cognitive growth of the infant, particularly when there are marked individual differences among infants for rates of cognitive growth. In the past, it was unacceptable to consider the importance of biological contributions to cognition because of the fact that cognitive measures have low predictive validity from one age to another during periods when cognitive changes are striking. The point was repeatedly made that, if there are biological contributions to cognitive development, such contributions should be evident early in life and that whatever individual differences are observed at that time should be steadfastly maintained thereafter. Numerous empirical studies of infant cognitive abilities seldom demonstrated robust stability coefficients, however. Therefore, the lack of stability for intervals as short as 6–12 months was considered to be evidence that the environment was largely or solely responsible for the rank order and reorder of infants from one age to the next.

By examining Bayley test scores obtained from infant twins followed longitudinally by the Louisville Twin Study, Wilson (1978) provided a different view of cognitive changes during infancy. He found that profiles of Bayley test scores generated across the ages of 3, 6, 9, 12, 18, and 24 months were matched more closely within monozygotic (MZ) pairs than within dizygotic (DZ) pairs. In effect, the variance of change in the rank order of individual differences from one age to the next could be attributed, at least in part, to genetic influences.

The years since Wilson's initial publications have seen major changes in the longitudinal study of infant twins. Among other things, there have been more twin studies launched, investigators have broadened the scope of assessments to include a variety of measures of cognition and other psychological constructs, sample sizes have increased so as to provide more statistical power, and more sophisticated methods for analysis have become readily available. These changes are clearly exemplified by the study reported in this *Monograph*.

The data and analyses presented herein are one of the products of ambitious efforts of a team of collaborators who initiated the MacArthur Longitudinal Twin Study in 1986. The MacArthur Twin Study was designed in such a way that twin pairs were tracked from the second year of infancy through early childhood; more recent developments for the MacArthur Twin Study, however, include following the twin pairs through the early years of formal schooling. Assessments of infants included measures of the major psychological constructs (cognition, emotion, and temperament, e.g.) and were scheduled at ages bracketing presumed transitions, inflections, or shifts in cognitive performance. At present, all twin pairs recruited by the MacArthur Twin Study have progressed beyond infancy, and the series of longitudinal assessments of infant twins has therefore been completed.

Although the rich data set from the MacArthur Twin Study could tempt one to incorporate all measures into a few overarching grand analyses, Reznick, Corley, and Robinson wisely restrict their analyses to but one general construct, cognition, as it develops during but one longitudinal span: from 14 to 20 to 24 months. The stated goal is exploratory or descriptive in nature, and sophisticated biometric modeling methods are applied for a multivariate, multimethod, longitudinal sample of twin pairs.

Questions of all sorts are anticipated by the investigators. To mention but a few, the *Monograph* addresses issues concerning sample, measures, methods for quantifying qualitative change, individual differences for cognitive development over three ages, sex differences, and the partitioning of variance into genetic and environmental components, the latter either shared by both twins within a pair or idiosyncratic to each twin. One cannot help but be awed by this thorough effort; the trade-off, however, is that one is confronted with a multiplicity of analyses providing a complex array of findings not easily reduced to a parsimonious theme for the development of cognition among infants. For example, sex differences are apparent for performance levels of the measures, for qualitative change of the measures, and for estimates of genetic and environmental influences. Reznick et al. are cautious about interpreting these sex differences; nevertheless, if these sex differences are replicated, one can envisage the creation of gender-specific models of cognitive growth akin to the gender-specific models applied to physical growth (Phillips & Matheny, 1990).

Given this somewhat untidy background of results, one has the prospect of picking through the complexities to find aspects that either enlighten or puzzle. To do so would reiterate much of the thoughtful discussion unfolding throughout the *Monograph*. Regardless, two aspects of the *Monograph* require comment.

Aspect of Measurement

It is a truism that the results from sophisticated multivariate techniques are constrained by the quality of the measures analyzed. For this *Monograph*, one measure, the Mental Development Index (MDI) from the Bayley Scales of Infant Development, is, from a psychometric perspective, exceptionally well constructed, highly reliable, and carefully standardized on broadly representative samples of children. The value of this test is augmented by the fact that it has been used extensively for research and clinical purposes, and its concurrent and predictive correlations are well known. Thereby, this test provides the touchstone for evaluating individual differences among infants and for quantifying relative changes in cognitive development. Perhaps for these reasons, a developmental-genetic analysis of continuity and change for the MDI obtained for the same infant twins sampled for this *Monograph* not only depended on the rigorous quality of the MDI but also yielded the same results (Cherny et al., 1994).

With one exception, one might also expect the three measures partially or wholly derived from the items of the MDI to have relatively sound psychometric properties. These measures—expressive language, receptive language, and nonverbal—essentially exhaust the pool of the MDI items appropriate for each of the three assessment ages. To create measures of expressive language and receptive language, additional items from the Sequenced Inventory of Communication Development were added. Appendix A of the *Monograph* provides an appreciation of the range of item difficulty for the measures, and it is apparent that the language composites, as well as the nonverbal composite, largely represent the range of item difficulty desired for sound construction of psychometric scales.

The one exception appears to be the expressive language measure at 14 months. In this instance, there is practically no spread of item difficulty because the pool of items represents a bifurcation: five of 16 items were scored correct for 80% or more of the infants, and 11 of 16 items were scored correct for fewer than 10% of the infants. Only one item among the 16 was in the mid-range for item difficulty. Should the apparent bifurcation of item difficulty yield a bimodal distribution of expressive language scores at 14 months, the scores may not be suitable for analyses based on the multivariate normal distribution. This may account for the intraclass correlations' being equivalent for both MZ and DZ pairs. It is likely that both twins within a pair, regardless of zygosity, will be found in the low (or high) end of the distribution of scores. Thereby, developmental-genetic analyses incorporating the expressive language measure at 14 months may not provide results as solid as portrayed.

More problematic are the measures included to assess specific cognitive characteristics. When compared with the verbal and nonverbal composites, word comprehension, visual attentiveness, and especially memory for locations are relatively unstable across ages and relatively less firmly correlated with MDI scores. Because all three measures provide systematic increases in level as test age progresses, and because all three measures appear to tap some cognitive competency, one understands why they were included in the assessment battery. Nevertheless, it now appears that they add "noise" to the interpretation of sources for the central theme of cognitive development in the second year of infancy.

Two of the specific cognitive measures, word comprehension and memory for locations, have quite large proportions of unshared variance unique or idiosyncratic to each infant. Reznick et al. offer a number of explanations for these idiosyncracies. While these explanations are plausible, it is also plausible that word comprehension and memory for locations are tasks highly specific to narrowly constrained cognitive competencies exercised within highly specific conditions. In this sense, it could be said that they represent more of a cognitive state than a trait. From a psychometric perspective, both measures may be more comparable to items or short subtests and are therefore less reliable.

Aspect of Interpretation

A guiding feature of the design of this study and the interpretive discussion is the notion of transition in the latter months of infancy. Reznick et al. allude to research from a number of sources as documenting a qualitative or quantitative change for infants' cognitive development during the interval between 18 and 24 months. For the most part, however, the empirical results are considered within the context of the research by McCall, Eichorn, and Hogarty (1977) and are interpreted accordingly.

McCall et al., along with a host of other researchers, have focused our attention on the remarkable change in an infant's display of cognitive (largely verbal) skills during the second year of life. Empirically, this has been demonstrated by showing that the major aspects of infant competencies change from sensorimotor, nonverbal skills to verbal skills. The change is illustrated by principal components and factor analyses of the items constituting tests of infant cognition. These analyses demonstrate that, during the infant's second year, and especially during the latter half, verbal items increasingly contribute to the first component or factor, which, in turn, concurrently correlates with total scores of cognition and predictively correlates with total scores from IQ tests. The results provided herein show an increasing relation between MDI scores and verbal measures during the interval from 14 to 24 months. To this extent, the results are indeed compatible with those of McCall et al. Implicitly, there has been a transition.

Unlike McCall et al., Reznick et al. do not offer a detailed specification of the timing of the transition. Because there were relatively few assessments and but few psychological constructs assessed, the time of transition is uncertain. This disclaimer is not persuasive, however, because it is not evident what would constitute crucial evidence for a transition. The essential problem for timing transitions, whether for this *Monograph,* or for McCall et al., or for anyone, is that *transition* can be defined in various ways, some of which are not easily verified empirically. For example, McCall et al. suggest that perturbation at 21 months in the quasi-simplex pattern of correlations for infant measures obtained at several ages in their study was an indication of a transition. The evidence is far from convincing, however, because the infants were eventually identified as being well above average for levels of IQ, cross-age correlations were based on small samples (typically about 20 infants), perturbations were not equivalent for girls and boys, and none of the differences described were tested for significance. One cannot help but wonder how these results could possibly generalize to larger, more typical populations of infants. If 21 months is indeed the transition age fixed for precocious infants, would not some later age for transition be more likely for infants less precocious?

Even if a perturbation in a quasi-simplex pattern is an acceptable operational definition, there remain problems when the definition is applied throughout development. For example, adolescence would certainly be an ideal period to look for transition(s) in view of the cognitive and physical changes that take place. Yet correlations for measures of IQ and height across ages spanning adolescence hardly vary around a remarkably high level of stability (Matheny, 1990). In this instance, a perturbation in a quasi-simplex correlation may not suffice to define *transition.*

A Piagetian view of transition pertains to a disequilibrium in the cognitive structure. Inconsistency in performance across cognitive tasks rather than instability of performance on a cognitive task across ages would be evidence for a transition. Possibly lower correlations among cognitive tasks at a given age, compared to previous and subsequent ages, would constitute an empirical test. If this is acceptable, then the results provided by Reznick et al. suggest that 14 months is more indicative of an age of transition than 20 or 24 months.

Other possible features for a transition could include a time when new behaviors abruptly emerge, when previous behaviors abruptly disappear, when behaviors become significantly repatterned or clustered, or when there is a learned acquisition of a culturally proscribed behavior. From the framework of developmental genetics, maybe a transition could be identified as the time when new genetic variation is found. Unfortunately, there is no clear way to decide what constitutes the determining features of a transition, particularly if the change involved is cited to be qualitative (Siegler & Richards, 1982).

Perhaps our acceptance of the notion of transition is no more than a convenience, a notion that helps us set apart one manageable package of cognitive development from another. For the developing structure of cognition, there may be no point of transition, just a segue.

References

Cherny, S. S., Fulker, D. W., Emde, R. N., Robinson, J., Corley, R. P., Reznick, J. S., Plomin, R., & DeFries, J. C. (1994). A developmental-genetic analysis of continuity and change in the Bayley Mental Development Index from 14 to 24 months: The MacArthur Longitudinal Twin Study. *Psychological Science, 5,* 354–360.

Matheny, A. P., Jr. (1990). Developmental behavior genetics: Contributions from the Louisville Twin Study. In M. R. Hahn, J. K. Hewitt, N. D. Henderson, & R. Benno (Eds.), *Developmental behavior genetics: Neural, biometrical, and evolutionary approaches.* New York: Oxford University Press.

McCall, R. B., Eichorn, D. H., & Hogarty, P. S. (1977). Transitions in early mental development. *Monographs of the Society for Research in Child Development, 42*(3, Serial No. 171).

Phillips, K., & Matheny, A. P., Jr. (1990). Quantitative genetic analysis of longitudinal trends in height: Preliminary results for the Louisville Twin Study. *Acta Geneticae Medicae et Gemellologiae, 39,* 143–163.

Siegler, R. S., & Richards, D. D. (1982). The development of intelligence. In R. J. Sternberg (Ed.), *Handbook of human intelligence.* New York: Cambridge University Press.

Wilson, R. S. (1978). Synchronies in mental development: An epigenetic perspective. *Science, 202,* 939–948.

CONTRIBUTORS

J. Steven Reznick (Ph.D. 1982, University of Colorado, Boulder) is associate professor of psychology at Yale University and the Yale Child Study Center. He is also a faculty member of the Bush Center in Child Development and the Yale Interdepartmental Neuroscience Program. He is on the editorial boards of *Developmental Psychology, Infant Behavior and Development, Cognitive Development, Developmental Science,* and the *General Psychology Review* and is a consulting editor for the *Infant Mental Health Journal.* His major research interests are in the area of cognitive development in human infants, particularly the development of representation and intentionality as reflected in memory, future-oriented behaviors, and language.

Robin Corley (Ph.D. 1987, University of Colorado, Boulder) is a research associate at the Institute for Behavioral Genetics, University of Colorado, Boulder. His research interests include the development and differentiation of specific cognitive abilities and the behavioral genetic analysis of traits manifesting homotypic and heterotypic continuity.

JoAnn Robinson (Ph.D. 1982, Cornell University) is formerly the research director of the MacArthur Longitudinal Twin Study and is currently assistant research professor of pediatrics and director of research for the Prevention Research Center for Family and Child Health at the University of Colorado Health Sciences Center. She is on the editorial board of *Developmental Psychology,* and her research focuses on early emotional development.

Adam P. Matheny Jr. (Ph.D. 1962, Vanderbilt University) is a professor of pediatrics at the University of Louisville and the director of the Louisville Twin Study. His current research pertains to twin studies of infant temperament, cognition, unintentional injuries of children, and home-environmental influences.

STATEMENT OF EDITORIAL POLICY

The *Monographs* series is intended as an outlet for major reports of developmental research that generate authoritative new findings and use these to foster a fresh and/or better-integrated perspective on some conceptually significant issue or controversy. Submissions from programmatic research projects are particularly welcome; these may consist of individually or group-authored reports of findings from some single large-scale investigation or of a sequence of experiments centering on some particular question. Multiauthored sets of independent studies that center on the same underlying question can also be appropriate; a critical requirement in such instances is that the various authors address common issues and that the contribution arising from the set as a whole be both unique and substantial. In essence, irrespective of how it may be framed, any work that contributes significant data and/or extends developmental thinking will be taken under editorial consideration.

Submissions should contain a minimum of 80 manuscript pages (including tables and references); the upper limit of 150–175 pages is much more flexible (please submit four copies; a copy of every submission and associated correspondence is deposited eventually in the archives of the SRCD). Neither membership in the Society for Research in Child Development nor affiliation with the academic discipline of psychology are relevant; the significance of the work in extending developmental theory and in contributing new empirical information is by far the most crucial consideration. Because the aim of the series is not only to advance knowledge on specialized topics but also to enhance cross-fertilization among disciplines or subfields, it is important that the links between the specific issues under study and larger questions relating to developmental processes emerge as clearly to the general reader as to specialists on the given topic.

Potential authors who may be unsure whether the manuscript they are planning would make an appropriate submission are invited to draft an outline of what they propose and send it to the Editor for assessment. This mechanism, as well as a more detailed description of all editorial policies, evaluation processes, and format requirements, is given in the "Guidelines for the Preparation of *Monographs* Submissions," which can be obtained by writing to the Editor, Rachel K. Clifton, Department of Psychology, University of Massachusetts, Amherst MA 01003.